RECLAIMING YOURSELF FROM BINGE EATING

THE WORKBOOK

Table of Contents

Pull-Outs and Worksheets

Reclaiming Yourself from Binge Eating Journal

This journal is meant to accompany _Reclaiming Yourself from Binge Eating: A Step-by-Step Guide to Healing._ All of the journal prompts from the book are included in this workbook in order to make your journey easier and meaningful. Each chapter corresponds with the chapters in the book. You will notice that there are skipped steps and chapters, that is because not each step in the book has a journal component to it.

Breaking free from binge eating is a beautiful journey that can be easy for some and more difficult for others. Whichever path is yours is okay. Sometimes we learn the most from our more difficult journeys.

Use your journal to take notice of what comes up for you during your process, write about your feelings and note ideas or thoughts that you want to return to later.

I hope that your journey is meaningful, healing and supportive.

STEP ONE: CREATING PURPOSE

Exercise One: Going Back in Time

If you could go back 15 years into the past, what would you tell your younger self? What lessons have you learned and what kind of changes would you make? Write a letter to your younger self, telling yourself exactly what you wish you wish that you had known then.

Writing Prompt:

Dear Self, I am coming to you from 15 years in the future to give you some valuable information:

_____

_____

_____

_____

_____

_____

_____

_____

_____

_____

_____

_____

_____

_____

_____

_____

_____

Now, close your eyes and try to imagine yourself 15 years in the future. If you were to continue traveling down the trajectory that you are on now, what kind of advice would your 15 year older self give your present self:

Writing Prompt:

Dear Self, if you continue to follow the path that you are currently on, this is where your life will be:

_____

_____

_____

_____

_____

_____

_____

_____

_____

_____

_____

_____

_____

_____

_____

_____

_____

_____

_____

_____

_____

_____

Here are some suggestions for loving and enriching ways continue on your path:

_____

_____

_____

_____

_____

_____

_____

_____

_____

_____

_____

_____

_____

_____

_____

_____

_____

_____

_____

_____

_____

_____

_____

_____

_____

_____

_____

Exercise Two: Why Should I Stop Binge Eating?

List every reason to quit binge eating:

_____

_____

_____

_____

_____

_____

_____

_____

_____

_____

_____

Now, make a list of reasons not to quit binge eating—this list is important. It helps you to understand your saboteurs. If there were absolutely no reason to continue doing it, you would have stopped a long time ago:

_____

_____

_____

_____

_____

_____

_____

_____

_____

_____

_____

Looking back at these letters and these lists, what do you notice?

_____

_____

_____

_____

_____

_____

_____

_____

_____

_____

Do your reasons for quitting binge eating outweigh your reasons for holding onto it?

_____

_____

_____

_____

_____

_____

_____

_____

_____

_____

_____

_____

Now, check out your reasons for not quitting binge eating. Look and see if you can challenge any of them:

Check out the following examples:

I don't want to quit binge eating because it's too hard:
Challenge Statement: It is hard that's true, but as I work to transform this habit, it will get easier. It takes time, dedication, and discipline, and I have the strength and the resources to do it. I know that I can't be perfect at something right off the bat, I have to practice. Even if it doesn't happen immediately, I am willing to practice this skill in order to give up binge eating.

I don't want to quit binge eating because it's the only thing that makes me feel better when I am sad:
Challenge Statement: Sometimes it makes me feel better, but often times it makes me feel worse. I also know that it's not true that the only thing that makes me feel better is binge eating, Sometimes talking on the phone to a friend helps, other times taking a walk outside, and still other times, renting a movie and watching it and zoning out in other non-food related ways can help.

What are **your** reasons?

I don't want to quit binge eating because:

_____

_____

_____

_____

_____

_____

_____

_____

Challenge Statement:

Try to come up with a challenge statement for every reason that you have not to quit binge eating.

_____

_____

_____

_____

_____

_____

_____

_____

_____

_____

_____

_____

Exercise Three: _Art Project!_

For this you will need either index cards, drawing paper, construction paper, or you can even use clay or sculpting materials. Go back to your reasons for wanting to quit binge eating. Write down each of those reasons on one side of the card or paper, and on the other side, draw a picture illustrating what that means to you. You can even mold or conceptualize your reasons. For instance, if you write, "I want to feel peaceful around food," draw a picture of yourself feeling peaceful or create a picture of what peace and calmness looks like to you. Or if you write, "I want to go places that I normally avoid because of food," draw a picture of yourself out in the world, enjoying your life and doing the things that you want to do. The next page is blank so that you can draw or sketch or fill it out as you please.

STEP TWO- Learn Intuitive Eating:

Exercise one: Exploring Your Feelings About Diets

Think about what is coming up for you around the ideas of giving up dieting. Example:

If I give up dieting I am afraid that:

I am afraid that I will gain so much weight that I won't be able to get out of bed.

I am afraid that I will gain so much weight that no one will want to talk to me and my partner won't be attracted to me.

I am afraid that I will lose my job and all of my friends, my husband will divorce me, no one will want to be with me and I'll be completely alone.

This makes me feel:

This makes me feel anxious. I am also angry that I am being asked to do this. This seems stupid and impossible.

What are the possible benefits of giving up dieting?

If I give up dieting, I might find that I have more fun when I go out. I might stop avoiding places that I've been avoiding and people who I've been avoiding. If I give up dieting, I might find that I can allow myself more of the kinds of food that I've been denying myself for so many years- except for when I'm bingeing. I might find that I feel more peaceful more of the time and less anxious around food.

I now feel:

A little calmer. I am still nervous, but I am willing to try giving up dieting for a few months and follow the protocol in this book. I am a little doubtful, yet I am hopeful. I'm willing to try anything at this point.

Now try answering these questions on your own, thinking about your own feelings:

If I give up dieting I am afraid that:

_____

_____

_____

_____

_____

_____

_____

_____

_____

_____

_____

This makes me feel:

_____

_____

_____

_____

_____

_____

_____

_____

_____

_____

_____

What are the possible benefits of giving up dieting?

_____
_____
_____
_____
_____
_____
_____
_____
_____
_____
_____
_____
_____

I now feel:

_____
_____
_____
_____
_____
_____
_____
_____
_____
_____
_____
_____
_____

Exercise Two: How Has Dieting Impacted My Life? This might help you to think more deeply about the cost/benefit analysis of giving up dieting. Ponder and answer the following questions.

How Long Have You Been Dieting?

_____

_____

_____

_____

What are the Various Types of Diets You Have Tried?

_____

_____

_____

_____

_____

_____

_____

What kinds of short-term results have these diets yielded?

_____

_____

_____

_____

_____

_____

_____

_____

What kinds of long-term results have these diets yielded?

_____

_____

_____

_____

_____

_____

_____

What has your life been like as a result of these diets?

_____

_____

_____

_____

_____

_____

_____

How would your life be different if dieting and food were not your focus?

_____

_____

_____

_____

_____

_____

_____

If you weren't dieting, what kinds of things would you be able to do that you currently feel you cannot?

_____

_____

_____

_____

_____

_____

_____

What kinds of places do you currently avoid because of your obsession with dieting, food, and body image?

_____

_____

_____

_____

_____

_____

_____

What would your life be like if you could do the things that you are currently avoiding?

_____

_____

_____

_____

_____

_____

_____

_____

What function does dieting serve for you?

_____

_____

_____

_____

_____

_____

_____

_____

_____

_____

_____

_____

How do you feel that dieting benefits you?

_____

_____

_____

_____

_____

_____

_____

_____

_____

_____

_____

How do you feel that dieting hurts you?

_____

_____

_____

_____

_____

_____

_____

_____

_____

_____

What would it be like if you could do the things you have been avoiding without having to think about food, dieting, or your body?

_____

_____

_____

_____

_____

_____

_____

_____

_____

_____

_____

STEP THREE: What's Behind the Urge to Binge Eat?

Exercise: Understanding Short Term Gains vs. Long Term Consequences

This exercise is designed to help you to understand why you binge eat, and what you hope to gain from it.

Short Term Gains: What are some short-term gains that you get from binge eating? Examples*:*

If I binge eat right now, I will not feel so lonely.

If I binge eat right now, I will not be sitting here obsessing about going to the store or going into the refrigerator or picking up the phone to order food.

If I binge eat right now, I will stop feeling so anxious or angry about something that recently happened.

If I binge eat right now, I can stop lying here having this argument with myself.

Write down some of your short-term gains from binge eating.

If I binge eat right now...

_____

_____

_____

_____

_____

_____

_____

_____

_____

_____

Long Term Consequences:

What are some of the longer-term consequences of binge eating? Think about how you will feel and what happens when you binge eat.

Examples:

If I binge eat, my stomach will hurt.

If I binge eat, I will fall asleep without getting anything done tonight.

If I binge eat, I will feel become overly full and bloated and feel uncomfortable in my body

If I binge eat, I will be angry with myself

What are some of your longer-term consequences of binge eating? Write down some of your own consequences of binge eating:

If I binge eat...

_____

_____

_____

_____

_____

_____

_____

_____

_____

_____

_____

_____

_____

_____

_____

_____

_____

_____

_____

STEP FOUR: Figuring Out Binge Triggers and How to Defeat Them

Exercise One: Alternative Action Log

Additional copies can be found at the end of the journal

Trigger: What Kind of Trigger was this, emotional, physical or situational?

_____

_____

_____

_____

Describe What Happened:

_____

_____

_____

_____

Feelings: (What am I feeling about it?)

_____

_____

_____

Short Term Solution: (What do I want to do in the short term to make me feel better?)

_____

_____

_____

Long Term Consequence: (How Will that make me feel later, or tomorrow?)

_____

_____

_____

_____

Alternative Behavior: (What else can I do to make myself feel better?)

_____

_____

_____

_____

Although this log is used to help keep you from bingeing, go back and write in it, even if you have already binged. This will help you to understand more about what you were feeling in the moment.

Exercise Two: Create a "Do Something Different" List

Write out a list of things that you can do to nurture yourself instead of binge eating. This is called a "Do Something Different List."

List as many alternatives to binge eating as you can think of. Begin by pondering what you would like to achieve by binge eating. Then think of something different that will help you achieve a similar feeling. Take that list, and perhaps paste it onto a beautiful, inspirational drawing and post it in a place where you will need it the most.

DO SOMETHING DIFFERENT

1. Get out of your home and take a walk if it is safe to do so.

2. Download music

3. Dance

4. Do Crossword puzzles

5. Call a friend, a family member, or a support person

7. Go to a bookstore

8. *Acknowledge your feelings and try to sit with them

9. Think about how you want to feel later -allow yourself to see your decision through to the end

10. Visualize something positive, like your life without an eating disorder

11. *Go to a support group meeting online or in person

12. Take a bath or a shower

13. Brush and floss your teeth

14. Light candles or incense

15. Lay down and rest or go to sleep if tired.

18. Read a book

19. Write a letter/email

20. Go through old letters or emails that make you feel better

21. Go through magazines and create a collage or vision board

22. Take out some art supplies and paint or draw

23. Do crafts

24. Do scrapbooking

25. Knit or teach yourself to knit or to sew

26. Go to church/synagogue

27. Watch a DVD or go out to the movies

28. Clean

29. Breath/meditate/stretch/do yoga

30. Bring food to homeless people in your neighborhood or to a local shelter

31. Volunteer or research volunteer opportunities

32. Go through your to-do list and begin to cross things off

33. Have a spa day in your home. Give yourself a hot oil treatment, manicure, pedicure and facial.

34. Go out and get a manicure. You can't eat with wet nails!

What are some things that help *you* feel good about yourself or help you feel warm and happy? Continue with your own list:

_____

_____

_____

_____

_____

_____

_____

_____

_____

_____

_____

Exercise Three: Understanding your Classical Conditioning

Do you notice patterns about when you overeat or binge?

_____

_____

_____

_____

_____

_____

Are there certain routines where you habitually overeat or binge? For example, right when you come home from work/school, or after going out at night?

_____

_____

_____

_____

_____

_____

_____

_____

What are some ways that you can break up your routine in the times that you typically binge?

_____

_____

_____

_____

_____

_____

_____

STEP FIVE: Self-Monitoring

Exercise One: Keep a Food and Mood Log

Additional copies can be found at the end of the journal

HOW DO YOU FEEL PHYSICALLY BEFORE EATING?

_____

_____

_____

HOW DO YOU FEEL EMOTIONALLY BEFORE EATING?

_____

_____

_____

DESCRIBE YOUR LEVEL OF HUNGER BEFORE EATING –USE H/S SCALE

_____

_____

_____

DESCRIBE WHAT YOU ATE INCLUDING SERVING SIZE:

_____

_____

_____

HOW DO YOU FEEL PHYSICALLY AFTER EATING?

_____

_____

_____

HOW DO YOU FEEL EMOTIONALLY AFTER EATING?

_____

_____

_____

DESCRIBE YOUR LEVEL OF HUNGER AFTER EATING:

_____

_____

_____

CHECK IN ONE HOUR LATER, HOW DO YOU FEEL NOW?

_____

_____

_____

_____

Now, as you analyze your food and mood log, answer the following questions:

What physical symptoms triggered disordered eating?

_____

_____

_____

_____

What emotional symptoms triggered disordered eating?

_____

_____

_____

_____

What could you have done differently to avoid a binge?

_____

_____

_____

_____

What patterns do you notice?

_____

_____

_____

_____

How many hours do you go between meals?

_____

_____

_____

_____

How do you feel when you're hungry?

_____

_____

_____

_____

How often do you let yourself get hungry?

_____

_____

_____

_____

What ways could you have taken care of yourself without using food?

_____

_____

_____

_____

Exercise Two: Face Your Trigger Foods

Create a list of trigger foods, foods that you notice you weren't able to stop eating after you started, or foods that brought on a binge of other foods. You might notice that your trigger food is something as innocuous as garbanzo beans. This isn't to judge, it is an honest "noticing" of where you need support.

Try to monitor for a week or two without making any changes. This will help you to better understand yourself and your motivations around food as well as your trigger foods, your trigger situations, your trigger emotions and your physical triggers. Once you do this, you deepen your understanding of what you need to help yourself recover.

_____

_____

_____

_____

_____

_____

_____

_____

_____

_____

_____

_____

_____

_____

_____

_____

_____

_____

_____

_____

_____

_____

STEP SEVEN: What Should I Be Eating?

Exercise: Make a list of 10-15 whole foods, a combination of protein (ie: meats, chicken, fish, eggs, dairy, nuts, or tofu) carbohydrates (ie: green vegetables, starchy vegetables, legumes, fruits and grains) and fats (oils, butter, nut butters) that you absolutely think of as low risk foods (foods you're not likely to binge on), and keep those in your house as staples.

_____

_____

_____

_____

_____

_____

_____

_____

_____

_____

_____

_____

_____

_____

_____

_____

_____

_____

_____

_____

STEP EIGHT: Plan on Eating Three Meals a Day

Exercise One: Create a Meal Plan

Create your own food plan and vow to follow it for just one day.

Meal Planner: *Additional copies can be found at the end of the journal*

Meal:	Time:	Place:	Planned Food:
_____	_____	_____	_____
_____	_____	_____	_____
_____	_____	_____	_____
_____	_____	_____	_____
_____	_____	_____	_____
_____	_____	_____	_____
_____	_____	_____	_____
_____	_____	_____	_____
_____	_____	_____	_____
_____	_____	_____	_____
_____	_____	_____	_____
_____	_____	_____	_____
_____	_____	_____	_____

Exercise Two: Figuring Out Why it's so hard to be a "normal" eater

I am/was afraid to implement a regular pattern of eating because:

_____

_____

_____

_____

_____

When I tried this one day experiment, I felt:

_____

_____

_____

_____

_____

Things that were hard about it were:

_____

_____

_____

_____

_____

Things that I liked about it were:

_____

_____

_____

_____

_____

In order to integrate a regular pattern of eating into my daily life, I need to:

_____

_____

_____

_____

_____

_____

STEP NINE: Understanding Your Hunger

Exercise: Learning What Real Hunger Feels Like In Your Body

Warning: Do not do this exercise without first consulting with your physician

Hunger/Satiety Scale can be found at the end of the journal

In preparation for this exercise, set aside a day when you don't have to go to work or have social plans. Find someone who will join you for the day to do things between journal sessions like watch movies or chat. Plan three non-binge meals that are each made up of protein, fat and carbohydrates. When you wake up in the morning, have a moderate breakfast. It is important that you do this on a day where you have not binged the night before. Try to include protein, fat, fiber, carbohydrates and vitamins in this breakfast. Something like 2 eggs scrambled with a bit of cheese, one piece of fruit, and one or two slices of whole grain toast with butter. After your meal, wait. At two hours, begin to check in with your body and notice if you have any signs of hunger. These signs might be your stomach growling, pain in your stomach, a feeling of emptiness, a lack of energy, fogginess, lack of concentration, headache, dizziness, obsessing about food, or other feelings. At the two hour mark, fill in the following chart:

Hunger Symptom	Do you have this? (yes/no)	If so, what number on hunger/satiety scale
Stomach Growling		
Stomach Pains		
Hollow Feelings		
Lack of Energy		
Fogginess		
Lack of Concentration		
Headache		
Dizziness		
Obsessing about Food		
Other Feelings		

Notice what you are feeling emotionally. In your journal, note what feelings are coming up for you. Are you feeling anxious about food? Are you feeling angry? Sad? What are you thinking about?

Now, wait another hour. When it's been three hours since you've eaten, begin to check your symptoms and mark them down:

Hunger Symptom	Do you have this? (yes/no)	If so, what number on hunger/satiety scale
Stomach Pains		
Hollow Feelings		
Lack of Energy		
Fogginess		
Lack of Concentration		
Headache		
Dizziness		
Obsessing about Food		
Other Feelings		

Notice what you are feeling emotionally. What feelings are coming up for you? Are you feeling anxious about food? Are you feeling angry? Sad? What are you thinking about? Another feeling that might be coming up for you around hunger is elation. For some people, the feeling of being empty is desirable. They might feel more in control, safer, and in some cases, morally superior.

Now, wait another hour. When it's been four hours since you've eaten, begin to check your symptoms and mark them down.

Hunger Symptom	Do you have this? (yes/no)	If so, what number on hunger/satiety scale
Stomach Pains		
Hollow Feelings		
Lack of Energy		
Fogginess		
Lack of Concentration		
Headache		
Dizziness		
Obsessing about Food		
Other Feelings		

Notice what you are feeling emotionally. What feelings are coming up for you? Are you feeling anxious about food? Are you feeling angry? Sad? What are you thinking about?

Now, wait another hour. When it's been five hours since you've eaten, begin to check your symptoms and mark them down.

Hunger Symptom	Do you have this? (yes/no)	If so, what number on hunger/satiety scale
Stomach Pains		
Hollow Feelings		
Lack of Energy		
Fogginess		
Lack of Concentration		
Headache		
Dizziness		
Obsessing about Food		
Other Feelings		

Notice what you are feeling emotionally. What feelings are coming up for you? Are you feeling anxious about food? Are you feeling angry? Sad? What are you thinking about?

At the six-hour mark, you should definitely be quite hungry. Allow yourself to check in one last time. At this point you should definitely understand what hunger feels like emotionally and physically. Check in again and mark off what you are feeling

physically and emotionally.

Hunger Symptom the scale?	Do you have this? (yes/no)	If so, what number on hunger/satiety
Stomach Pains		
Hollow Feelings		
Lack of Energy		
Fogginess		
Lack of Concentration		
Headache		
Dizziness		
Obsessing about Food		
Other Feelings		

What feelings are coming up for you?

_____

_____

_____

_____

_____

_____

Are you feeling anxious about food? Explain:

_____

_____

_____

_____

_____

_____

Are you feeling angry? Explain:

_____

_____

_____

_____

_____

_____

Sad? Explain:

_____

_____

_____

_____

_____

_____

What are you thinking about?

_____

_____

_____

_____

_____

_____

At this point, allow yourself to eat a full non-binge meal. Try to eat slowly and to notice as you go from being hungry to being satisfied. Because you are so hungry and because you might have lots of emotions coming up for you from this exercise, you might find that you have the instinct to eat very quickly to make the hunger and the feelings disappear. Slow yourself down and notice what truly satisfying your hunger feels like. Try to stop when you are at a 6, when you are satisfied, but not full. As you continue on your journey, each meal should start at a 3 and end by a 6 or 7.

You should not end your meals by saying, "I'm so full," you should feel sated and nourished.

Exercise Four: Understanding the cues that cause you to eat

The next time you eat anything, sit down afterwards and answer these questions:

Were you physically hungry?

_____

_____

If you were physically hungry, how did you know that? What were the bodily cues that told you to eat?

_____

_____

_____

_____

_____

_____

Were you psychologically hungry?

_____

_____

If you were psychologically hungry, what were you hungry for? What did you need emotionally? Were you bored, tired, angry, lonely? What else could have fed you?

_____

_____

_____

_____

_____

_____

Were you eating as a conditioned response? For example, popcorn at a movie, or snack after work?

_____

_____

_____

_____

_____

_____

_____

_____

_____

_____

_____

If so, is there a way that you could notice this in the future? How?

_____

_____

_____

_____

_____

_____

_____

_____

_____

_____

_____

_____

_____

STEP TEN: Overpowering your Urge to Binge

Exercise One: Personifying your Bingeing

The point of this exercise is to help you to gain some power over your binge eating. By externalizing your binge eating and recognizing that it is not an inseparable part of yourself, you are able to detach yourself from the disorder. Some people think that they are a walking eating disorder, but you are not. You are a whole, solid human being with an issue that needs attention and a behavior that you'd like to extinguish. You are not hopeless.

Answer the following questions:

What is the name of your binge monster? Think about the parasite that comes and has you bingeing before you even believe that you have a choice, what will you call this entity? _____

What does it look like? Describe it in words:_____
_____
_____
_____
_____

How long has it been living on you/in you? _____

When did she or he first attach himself/herself onto you? How old were you? What were the circumstances surrounding it?_____
_____
_____

Draw a Picture of your binge monster (next page intentionally left blank):

Write a letter to your binge monster letting it know how you feel about it. Ask it what its purpose is, and why it has chosen to come to you.

_____

_____

_____

_____

_____

_____

_____

_____

_____

_____

_____

_____

_____

_____

_____

_____

_____

_____

_____

_____

_____

_____

_____

_____

_____

Write a letter to yourself from your binge monster to you explaining why he or she is there, and whatever else it wants you to know.

Write a letter back to your binge monster explaining why you don't need him or her, and what coping mechanisms you have to deal with life other than him or her.

_____

_____

_____

_____

_____

_____

_____

_____

_____

_____

_____

_____

_____

_____

_____

_____

_____

_____

_____

_____

_____

_____

_____

_____

_____

_____

_____

_____

STEP TWELVE: Balancing Self-Acceptance with the Need to Change

Exercise One: Self-Acceptance

Complete the following sentence:

I am afraid of accepting myself as I am because: _____

_____

_____

_____

_____

_____

If I were to accept my body shape, I might feel:_____

_____

_____

_____

_____

_____

_____

_____

_____

If I were to accept my eating issues, I might feel: _____

_____

_____

_____

_____

_____

_____

_____

_____

The Bad thing about accepting my eating issues is:_____

_____

_____

_____

_____

_____

The Bad thing about accepting my body shape is: _____

_____

_____

_____

_____

_____

A positive thing that might happen if I accept my eating issues is: _____

_____

_____

_____

_____

_____

_____

A good thing that might happen if I accept my body shape is: _____

_____

_____

_____

_____

_____

Exercise Three: Finding positive qualities

Make a list of things that you like about yourself and what you feel your positive qualities are:

_____

_____

_____

_____

_____

_____

_____

Make a list of things that you don't like about yourself and what you feel your negative qualities are:

_____

_____

_____

_____

_____

_____

_____

Do your bad qualities make you a bad person? Why or Why Not?

_____

_____

_____

_____

_____

_____

Do your bad qualities take away from your good qualities? Why or Why Not?

_____

_____

_____

_____

_____

_____

_____

_____

_____

Can you accept that you have both bad and good qualities?

_____

_____

_____

_____

Why or Why Not?

_____

_____

_____

_____

_____

_____

_____

_____

_____

STEP THIRTEEN: Retroflecting

Exercise One: Are you hurting yourself when you feel angry at someone else?

Think about a time when you might have reacted to someone else by binge eating. Answer the following questions:

Has there ever been a time when someone did something and said something that made you feel totally helpless? _____

_____

_____

_____

_____

If so, what happened? What did this person do or say?_____

_____

_____

_____

_____

_____

_____

How did you react emotionally? (How did you feel?)_____

_____

_____

_____

_____

_____

_____

How did you react behaviorally? (What actions did you carry out in reaction to this?) _____

_____

_____

_____

_____

_____

In thinking about this situation, was there a better way that you could have behaved?_____

_____

_____

_____

_____

_____

_____

Exercise Two: Letting Go of Control of another person or situation

Name a person or situation that is currently occurring that is causing you to feel powerless, hopeless, or out of control: _____

_____

_____

_____

Is there any part of this situation that you can control? How can you do that?_____

_____

_____

_____

_____

Which part do you have no control over? _____

_____

_____

_____

_____

Admitting and understanding that you have no control over this person or situation, what can you do to soothe and take care of yourself?

_____

_____

_____

_____

_____

_____

Write a letter to this person or to the situation letting them know exactly what you're feeling. Don't hold back with this letter, let everything that you feel come out. Then, allow yourself to take the letter and either burn it, or even put it in a bottle and send it out to sea.

_____

_____

_____

_____

_____

_____

_____

_____

_____

STEP FOURTEEN: Dealing with Self-Sabotage

Exercise: How are You Self Sabotaging by Binge Eating?

I am afraid that if I stop binge eating:

_____

_____

_____

_____

I am afraid that if I don't stop binge eating:

_____

_____

_____

_____

_____

_____

Some of the ways I sabotage myself with food are by:

_____

_____

_____

_____

_____

_____

_____

_____

_____

Some other ways that I sabotage myself in life are by:

_____

_____

_____

_____

_____

_____

_____

_____

If I stopped self-sabotaging with food, what might happen?

_____

_____

_____

_____

_____

_____

_____

_____

If I stopped self-sabotaging in other ways, what might happen?

_____

_____

_____

_____

_____

_____

What are some ways that I can stop myself from sabotaging my good intentions?

_____

_____

_____

_____

_____

_____

_____

_____

_____

Who are some people who will help support me with my goals?

_____

_____

_____

_____

_____

_____

_____

Discuss with the people above what your goals are. Of course these should be safe people. Let them know what you are working on and how you've been sabotaging. Ask them if you can be accountable to them. This does not mean that they are supposed to push you or make you do the things that you want to do, it just means that they are there to listen to your goals and to listen to what happened when you self sabotaged.

STEP FIFTEEN: Dealing with Procrastination

Exercise: Ending Procrastination and Getting Moving

What is something that you often find yourself procrastinating on?

_____

_____

How do you feel about this particular task?

_____

_____

_____

How do you feel while you are doing this task?

_____

_____

_____

_____

How do you feel while you're thinking about this task?

_____

_____

_____

_____

How does food help you when you are procrastinating?

_____

_____

_____

_____

What are your fears about doing this task?

_____

_____

_____

_____

What are your fears about not doing this task?

_____

_____

_____

_____

Whenever you find yourself procrastinating about something, use the procrastination worksheet at the end of the journal to help you sort through it.

You might notice through this exercise that the task itself feels bigger than it actually is because you've created much more out of it than the simple task that it is.

STEP SIXTEEN- Dealing With Boredom

Exercise: Understanding Your Boredom

Do you ever eat out of boredom?_____

_____

_____

When do you find that you are the most bored? _____

_____

_____

If you weren't bored, what would you be thinking about? (What's underneath the

boredom?)_____

_____

_____

Do you think that you use boredom as a substitution for anything? If so, what is
that?

_____

_____

_____

_____

How does eating help you when you're bored? _____

_____

_____

_____

_____

How does eating when you're bored hurt you?_____

_____

_____

_____

_____

Are there other ways that you can nurture yourself when you are bored? If so, what

are they?_____

_____

_____

_____

_____

Are there other things that you can look forward to besides food? If so, what are

they?_____

_____

_____

_____

_____

_____

_____

_____

_____

_____

_____

_____

_____

_____

STEP SEVENTEEN- Sleep Issues and Night Eating

Exercise One: Battling Night Eating

Each night before you go to bed, sit down with your journal and begin to write the Before Bed Journal can be found at the end of the journal. Here are some prompts to get you started:

I think:_____

_____

_____

_____

_____

I need: _____

_____

_____

_____

_____

I feel: _____

_____

_____

_____

_____

_____

Today I:_____

_____

_____

_____

_____

I wish that:_____

_____

_____

_____

_____

The worst part of my day today was: _____

_____

_____

_____

The best part of my day today was: _____

_____

_____

_____

Anything Else I need to sort through: _____

_____

_____

_____

STEP EIGHTEEN- What Do you Binge On?

Exercise: Considering Your Binge Foods

What are your binge foods?_____

_____

_____

_____

_____

_____

_____

Do you have favorites? _____

_____

_____

_____

Think about what individual purpose they might be serving. What are you feeling when you're bingeing? Are you feeling frustrated? Anxious? Do you need comfort? Love? Sweetness in your life? Are you feeling empty? Bored? Think about what you eat and how it relates to why you do what you do.

_____

_____

_____

_____

_____

_____

_____

_____

_____

STEP NINETEEN- How to Soothe Yourself Through Uncomfortable Feelings

Exercise One: Understanding your Automatic Thoughts and How they Affect your Feelings

Automatic Thought Log

Additional copies can be found at the end of the journal

Think about a time when you were feeling very upset about something that happened.

What are you feeling?_____

_____

_____

_____

_____

_____

_____

On a scale from 1-10, how strong are these feelings?_____

Give three thoughts that are triggering these feelings?_____

_____

_____

_____

_____

_____

_____

For each of these statements, what is absolutely true?_____

_____

_____

_____

How do you know that's true?_____

_____

_____

_____

_____

_____

_____

Are there any thoughts here that might not be true?_____

_____

_____

_____

_____

_____

_____

How do you know that these thoughts might not be true?_____

_____

_____

_____

_____

_____

_____

What is a more balanced truth here?_____

_____

_____

_____

_____

_____

_____

What kind of cognitive distortion is this? _____

_____

_____

_____

_____

_____

_____

How are you feeling now?_____

_____

_____

_____

_____

_____

_____

On a scale from 1-10, how strong are these feelings now?_____

You can use the automatic thought log any time you are feeling caught up in your
head and unable to escape from your thoughts, or anytime you are just feeling
distressed and needing some help out of that dangerous neighborhood.

STEP TWENTY- Healing Shame

Exercise One: Breaking Away from Shaming Friends or Acquaintances

Make a list of people whom you feel either inferior to or badly about yourself when you are around them:

_____

_____

_____

_____

_____

_____

_____

_____

_____

Who are some people that you like yourself when you're around?

_____

_____

_____

_____

_____

_____

_____

_____

_____

What reasons do you have for spending time with the first list of people?

_____

_____

_____

_____

_____

_____

What are some ways that you can create limits with the first group of people and increase your time with the second group?

_____

_____

_____

_____

_____

_____

Exercise Two: Understanding Your Family Patterns of Shame

Did you or do you feel badly about yourself around your parents?_____

_____

_____

_____

What things did your parents say or do to cause you to feel badly about yourself?

_____

_____

_____

_____

_____

_____

How are these things still with you?

_____

_____

_____

Your parents probably held these beliefs and acted this way because:_____

_____

_____

_____

_____

_____

_____

Just because these messages came from your parents, does that necessarily mean that they are true? Why or why not?

_____

_____

_____

Is it okay for you to make the choice not to accept this shaming message?

_____

_____

_____

What are some new, non-shaming messages that you can integrate into your psyche?

_____

_____

_____

_____

What are some ways that you can allow yourself to feel these new messages?

_____

_____

_____

_____

_____

_____

_____

_____

Exercise Three: Challenging Omniscient Internal Shame

Below are some common self-limiting thoughts that perpetuate shame.

Check those that apply to you and explore where this belief came from, then write your own challenge statement.

There is an example after each one. You can use that one, or you can write one that is more pertinent to your situation.

Self-Limiting Thought: I must always be doing something, I am nothing if I am not constantly productive

Do you have this belief? If so, what do you think led you to believe this?

_____

_____

_____

_____

When do you first remember feeling this way?

_____

_____

_____

_____

Shameful Belief: Being productive is what gives me value.

Challenge Statement: The person I am is already valuable.

What are some other positive beliefs you might have?

_____

_____

_____

How can you practice and integrate the positive beliefs?

_____

_____

_____

_____

Self-Limiting Thought: I must always be perfect

Do you have this belief? If so, what do you think led you to believe this?

_____

_____

_____

_____

When do you first remember feeling this way?

_____

_____

_____

_____

Shameful Belief: I always have to be perfect no matter what.

Challenge Statement: I am a human being, with perfectly human flaws. I make mistakes sometimes and that is okay.

What are some other positive beliefs you might have?

_____

_____

_____

_____

How can you practice and integrate the positive beliefs?

_____

_____

_____

_____

Self-Limiting Thought: I never do anything right

Do you have this belief? If so, what do you think led you to believe this?

_____

_____

_____

_____

When do you first remember feeling this way?

_____

_____

_____

_____

Shameful Belief: I can only fantasize about what I want, in real life though, things don't ever go my way.

Challenge Statement: I create my own destiny and I have the power to do what I want to do; the only person who has the power to stop me is me. I am choosing to go forward, not stop myself.

What are some other positive beliefs you might have?

_____

_____

_____

_____

How can you practice and integrate the positive beliefs?

_____

_____

_____

_____

When you think about your eating issues, what defeating thoughts do you have?

_____

_____

_____

_____

What are some ways to challenge these defeating thoughts?

_____

_____

_____

_____

Self-Limiting Thought: I have to be smaller, stronger, faster and smarter than everyone. Nothing less is acceptable.

Do you have this belief? If so, what do you think led you to believe this?

_____

_____

_____

_____

When do you first remember feeling this way?

_____

_____

_____

_____

How are your overachieving beliefs tied in with food and your body?

_____

_____

_____

_____

Shameful Belief: I am not doing enough, I have to do more, do better and be the best.

Challenge Statement: I am doing what I can and allowing myself to enjoy myself and my life while I am doing it.

What are some other positive beliefs you might have? How can you practice and integrate the positive beliefs?

_____

_____

_____

_____

What are some ways that you can balance liking and nurturing yourself while still being goal-oriented?

_____

_____

Self-Limiting Thought: I am a worthless human being

Do you have this belief? If so, what do you think led you to believe this?

_____

_____

_____

_____

When do you first remember feeling this way?

_____

_____

_____

_____

How have your food issues and body image issues played in to this belief?

_____

_____

_____

_____

Shameful Belief: Who I am is not very important. In order for me to be valid, I have to make sure that I am doing things for other people constantly. If not, I'm worthless.

Challenge Statement: I am a worthwhile person just because of who I am. I don't have to give all of myself to people in order to be valid in the world.

What are some other positive beliefs you might have?

_____

_____

_____

_____

How can you practice and integrate the positive beliefs?

_____

_____

_____

_____

There are some great things that I do appreciate most about myself. Like:

_____

_____

_____

_____

_____

_____

_____

Self-Limiting Thought: I am responsible for everything and everyone around me

Do you have this belief? If so, what do you think led you to believe this?

_____

_____

_____

_____

When do you first remember feeling this way?

_____

_____

_____

_____

Shameful Belief: I always have to be in control of the situation and make sure that I am taking care of everyone and everything.

Challenge Statement: I am not responsible for anyone's actions or reactions except for my own. I only have to deal with my own emotions and allow space for each person to take care of themselves.

What are some other positive beliefs you might have?

_____

_____

_____

_____

How can you practice and integrate the positive beliefs?

_____

_____

_____

_____

These are the people and situations that I am always trying to control:

_____

_____

_____

_____

I understand that these things are beyond my control and I am willing to let go of them by doing the following:

_____

_____

_____

_____

Self-Limiting Thought: It's not okay for me to set boundaries

Do you have this belief? If so, what do you think led you to believe this?

_____

_____

_____

_____

When do you first remember feeling this way?

_____

_____

_____

_____

How have your food issues and body image issues played in to this belief?

_____

_____

_____

_____

Shameful Belief: I have no choice than to do whatever you want or need me to do.

Challenge Statement: My life is my own. It is my responsibility and my right to say "no" and to do whatever feels safe for me, no matter what it is.

What are some other positive beliefs you might have?

_____

_____

_____

_____

How can you practice and integrate the positive beliefs?

_____

_____

_____

_____

Who are some of the people and/or situations in your life that you need to say "no" to or set boundaries with?

_____

_____

_____

_____

The next time someone asks you to do something, ask yourself the following question: "If I don't do this will I feel guilty? If I do this will I feel resentful?" If the answer is yes, this is probably a good opportunity for you to try to set boundaries and say "no" or come up with a mutually beneficial compromise. There are of course times when you will say yes and want to do what the other person asks you for. There will also be times when you don't want to say yes but, for certain circumstances, you have obligations that you must follow through on. For instance, you have obligations to your children, or sick family members or friends or for someone who has also been generous with her time and energy. It's important to understand the law of reciprocity here. Allow yourself to give, but also to receive. If you are the only one giving, there is no balance.

Are there places in your life where the balance should be restored? Where?

_____

_____

_____

_____

How can you make that change?

_____

_____

_____

_____

How have food and your body been unbalanced? How can you change that?

_____

_____

_____

_____

Self-Limiting Thought: I am a slacker

Do you have this belief? If so, what do you think led you to believe this?

_____

_____

_____

_____

How does this belief about yourself relate to food and your body image?

_____

_____

_____

_____

When do you first remember feeling this way?

_____

_____

_____

_____

Shameful Belief: I have no ability to improve my life.

Challenge Statement: I have the power to create the life that I want for myself. I am not powerless. I am capable and strong.

What are some other positive beliefs you might have?

_____

_____

_____

_____

How can you practice and integrate the positive beliefs?

_____

_____

_____

_____

What are some of the failures that you've had?

_____

_____

_____

_____

How can you apply this to food and your body?

_____

_____

_____

_____

What are some accomplishments that you've had?

_____

_____

_____

_____

What are some things in your life that you've always wanted to do that you've always been too afraid of?

_____

_____

_____

_____

_____

_____

_____

_____

Self-Limiting Thought: Everyone should like me

Do you have this belief? If so, what do you think led you to believe this?

_____

_____

_____

_____

When do you first remember feeling this way?

_____

_____

_____

_____

How does this relate to food and your body image?

_____

_____

_____

_____

Shameful Belief: I need to do whatever I can to please people around me.

Challenge Statement: I am fine just the way I am even if some people don't like or approve of me. Liking myself is what matters the most. I don't need other people to tell me whether or not it's okay to do that.

What are some other positive beliefs you might have?

_____

_____

_____

_____

How can you practice and integrate the positive beliefs?

_____

_____

_____

_____

Something that I like about myself or want to do more of, that other people might not like or approve of, is:

_____

_____

_____

_____

What might happen if I did these things that certain people in my life did not approve of?

_____

_____

_____

_____

What are some ways that I can get support and deal with that?

_____

_____

_____

_____

Self-Limiting Thought: I am terrified that people will leave me or reject me

Do you have this belief? If so, what do you think led you to believe this?

_____

_____

_____

_____

When do you first remember feeling this way?

_____

_____

_____

_____

Shameful Belief: People will inevitably abandon me and I will always be alone.

Challenge Statement: I am perfect, whole and complete exactly as I am. People want to be around me and won't abandon me.

What are some other positive beliefs you might have?

_____

_____

_____

_____

How can you practice and integrate the positive beliefs?

_____

_____

_____

_____

Are there people in your life who are rejecting and abandoning? _____
If so, who are they?

_____

_____

_____

_____

Is it necessary for you to keep working to ensure that these people will stay with you?

_____

_____

_____

_____

Why or why not?

_____

_____

_____

_____

Are there some people in your life who you feel safe and secure with?

_____

_____

_____

_____

How do you know that they won't abandon you?

_____

_____

_____

_____

What are some ways that they have led you to believe that they are not planning on abandoning you?

_____

_____

_____

_____

Self-Limiting Thought: Conflict is not okay and I must avoid it at all costs

Do you have this belief? If so, what do you think led you to believe this?

_____

_____

_____

_____

When do you first remember feeling this way?

_____

_____

_____

_____

Shameful Belief: I should keep my mouth shut no matter how I'm feeling about a situation.

Challenge Statement: My thoughts and feelings are valid and important, and it's okay for me to talk about things that bother me open and honestly.

What are some other positive beliefs you might have?

_____

_____

How can you practice and integrate the positive beliefs?

_____

_____

_____

_____

What are some conflicts that you try to avoid?

_____

_____

_____

_____

Do you ever use food to push down your feelings when you avoid conflict? If so, how?

_____

_____

_____

_____

What might happen if you didn't avoid these conflicts?

_____

_____

_____

_____

Self-Limiting Thought: People can't know who I really am or the things I really think about or do

Do you have this belief? If so, what do you think led you to believe this?

_____

_____

_____

_____

When do you first remember feeling this way?

_____

_____

_____

_____

Shameful Belief: It's not okay for me to be having these feelings. My feelings are wrong. People can't think that I have feelings such as sadness, anger or loneliness. People can't know the shameful things I do to cope with these feelings.

Challenge Statement: It's normal and human for me to have varying ranges of emotions, thoughts, habits and coping mechanisms. Everyone does and it is okay for people to see the real me. I don't have to use unhealthy coping mechanisms or be alone with this; I can get support and help from others out there dealing with similar issues.

What are some other positive beliefs you might have?

_____

_____

_____

_____

How can you practice and integrate the positive beliefs?

_____

_____

_____

_____

What are some ways that you reject your true self?

_____

_____

_____

_____

How can you practice accepting your true self?

_____

_____

_____

_____

What would it be like to start showing people who you really are?

_____

_____

_____

_____

Is there anything that scares you about doing that? If so, what is it?

_____

_____

_____

_____

What would be the possible negative consequences of showing people your true authentic self?

_____

_____

_____

_____

What would be the possible positive consequences of showing people your true authentic self?

_____

_____

_____

_____

Self-Limiting Thought: I don't have any needs

Do you have this belief? If so, what do you think led you to believe this?

_____

_____

_____

_____

When do you first remember feeling this way?

_____

_____

_____

_____

Shameful Belief: It is never okay for me to have any needs, if I do I am needy. I have to be completely fine all the time.

Challenge Statement: Human beings are interdependent. We all have needs and it's okay for me to express those needs and trust that there are certain people who will meet them.

What are some other positive beliefs you might have?

_____

_____

_____

_____

How can you practice and integrate the positive beliefs?

_____

_____

_____

_____

What kinds of needs do you have that you feel unsafe expressing?

_____

_____

_____

_____

Do you ever suppress your need for food in order to feel better or more virtuous?

_____

_____

What unmet needs have you been suppressing?

_____

_____

_____

_____

Who do you feel safe expressing your needs to?

_____

_____

_____

_____

How can you start to do this?

_____

_____

_____

_____

Self-Limiting Thought: I am a total loser

Do you have this belief? If so, what do you think led you to believe this?

_____

_____

_____

_____

When do you first remember feeling this way?

_____

_____

_____

_____

Shameful Belief: It's not okay for me to be me. I have to change in order to be okay.

Challenge Statement: I am fine the way I am. I'm just fine. As long as I am a kind human being and hold myself with integrity, I know that I'll be okay. I don't have to be anything other than the great person that I am.

What are some other positive beliefs you might have?

_____

_____

_____

_____

How can you practice and integrate the positive beliefs?

_____

_____

_____

_____

What are some things that you like about yourself?

_____

_____

_____

_____

What makes you valuable as a human being?

_____

_____

_____

_____

Who believes in you and cherishes you?

_____

_____

_____

_____

How can you start to internalize their voice of love for yourself?

_____

_____

_____

_____

_____

_____

_____

_____

_____

_____

_____

_____

_____

_____

STEP TWENTY-ONE: Dealing with your Inner Critic and Gaining Self-Esteem

Exercise One: Meeting the Inner Critic:

Additional copies of the inner critic worksheet can be found at the end of the journal

At the beginning of healing your critic, you might find it too challenging to confront your critic or to challenge it. That's okay. Start off slowly just by acknowledging it and separating it. For a couple of days, each time your critic says something to you, write it down.

Example:

Date & Time: *2/14 8:30am*

Event or Trigger (what happened): *I was trying to get dressed in the morning and couldn't find anything to wear*

What my Critic Said: *You look fat and ugly in all your clothes, everyone is going to feel sorry for your because you're single on Valentine's Day. Everything you put on makes you look like a pink pig. You might as well stay home and eat chocolate all day long.*

How that Made Me Feel: *I felt miserable and powerless and anxious because I had to get to work but I was paralyzed. I couldn't do anything.*

How I reacted or behaved in reaction to this: *I laid on the floor and cried and wound up getting into work 20 minutes late.*

Date & Time:_____

Event or Trigger (what happened):_____

_____

_____

_____

_____

_____

_____

_____

_____

_____

What my Critic Said: _____

_____

_____

_____

_____

How that Made Me Feel:_____

_____

_____

_____

_____

How I reacted or behaved in reaction to this:_____

_____

_____

_____

_____

Exercise Two: Getting to know your Inner Critic

Now that you've met your inner critic, let's get to know who this is. Begin by taking some space to draw a picture of your Inner Critic, you can also color, sculpt, sketch or paint your critic. Then, give your critic a name. Next, explore the following prompts in your journal:

I find (name of inner critic) _____helpful because:

_____

_____

_____

_____

_____

_____

I am afraid of letting go of _____ because:

_____

_____

_____

_____

_____

_____

A positive result of letting go of _____ might be:

_____

_____

_____

_____

_____

_____

This is how I imagine I might feel if I let go of _____:

_____

_____

_____

_____

_____

_____

Something that _____ often tells me is:

_____

_____

_____

_____

_____

_____

The first time I heard this criticism was from **this person**_____

during **this situation**_____:

_____

_____

_____

_____

_____

_____

My mother often criticized me: True or False

If so, how?

_____

_____

_____

_____

_____

_____

My father often criticized me: True or False

If so, how?

_____

_____

_____

_____

_____

_____

My mother often criticized herself or others: True or False

If so, how?

_____

_____

_____

_____

_____

_____

My father often criticized himself or others: True or False

If so, how?

_____

_____

_____

_____

_____

_____

My mother often criticized my father: True or False

If so, how?

_____

_____

_____

_____

_____

_____

My father often criticized my mother: True or False

If so, how?

_____

_____

_____

_____

_____

_____

One very critical person I remember being around was: _____

They often did or said this:

_____

_____

_____

_____

_____

_____

Exercise Three: Learning to talk to your Inner Critic

Draw a picture of your Inner nurturer, you can also color, sculpt, sketch or paint your nurturer. (next page intentionally left blank):

What is your nurturer's name? _____

What does your inner nurturer mean to you? How can he/she help you?

_____

_____

_____

_____

_____

_____

_____

_____

_____

_____

_____

_____

_____

_____

_____

_____

_____

_____

_____

_____

Draw a picture of your Inner Cheerleader, you can also color, sculpt, sketch or paint your cheerleader.

What does your inner cheerleader mean to you? How can he/she help you?

_____

_____

_____

_____

_____

_____

If I overeat, my critic says to me:

_____

_____

_____

_____

If I had one, my inner nurturer would then respond:

_____

_____

_____

_____

If I had one, my inner cheerleader would encourage me by saying:

_____

_____

_____

_____

If I think that I've said something stupid, my critic tells me:

_____

_____

_____

_____

If I had one, my inner nurturer would then respond:

_____

_____

_____

_____

If I had one, my inner cheerleader would encourage me by saying:

_____

_____

_____

_____

If I have hurt someone's feelings, my critic tells me:

_____

_____

_____

_____

If I had one, my inner nurturer would then respond:

_____

_____

_____

_____

If I had one, my inner cheerleader would encourage me by saying:

_____

_____

_____

_____

If I make a mistake at work or in school, my critic says to me:

_____

_____

_____

_____

If I had one, my inner nurturer would then respond:

_____

_____

_____

_____

If I had one, my inner cheerleader would encourage me by saying:

_____

_____

_____

_____

If I notice that I have put on some weight, my critic says to me:

_____

_____

_____

_____

If I had one, my inner nurturer would then respond:

_____

_____

_____

_____

If I had one, my inner cheerleader would encourage me by saying:

_____

_____

_____

_____

If I accidentally overdraw my bank account, my critic says to me:

_____

_____

_____

_____

If I had one, my inner nurturer would then respond:

_____

_____

_____

_____

If I had one, my inner cheerleader would encourage me by saying:

_____

_____

_____

_____

Now, in your journal, create some responses for other things that your critic might say to you.

Critic: Don't talk, if you do, surely you will say the wrong thing and everyone will think that you are stupid,

Your Response:

_____

_____

_____

_____

Critic: You fat pig, you better not eat anything today.

Your Response:

_____

_____

_____

_____

Critic: No one will ever want to date you until you lose the weight

Your Response:

_____

_____

_____

_____

Critic: You have one month until that wedding, you need to lose 20 pounds in that time. What crash diet can you go on?

Your Response:

_____

_____

_____

_____

Critic: You are not smart or good looking enough to spend time with those people.

Your Response:

_____

_____

_____

_____

STEP TWENTY-TWO: Being Kind to Yourself

Affirmation Maker *Additional copies can be found at the end of the journal*

The Goal You Want to Accomplish	The Affirmation to Help you Get there	The Eventual Affirmation

STEP TWENTY-THREE: Letting Go of Polarized Thinking

Exercise One: Integrating Flexible Thinking

Try to imagine some flexible thinking options for each would scenario:

You are at a restaurant with a friend and you vow not to eat any bread. However, the dinner rolls come out and despite your best efforts to restrain yourself, you wind up eating one.

What is the all or nothing thinking?

_____

_____

_____

What are some flexible thinking options?

_____

_____

_____

You are planning on wearing a particular pair of pants to a party. However, on the night of the party, you realize that the pants feel a bit too tight.

What is the all or nothing thinking?

_____

_____

_____

_____

What are some flexible thinking options?

_____

_____

_____

_____

You go to a party and decide not to drink any alcohol that night. However, you give in eventually and have a glass of wine.

What is the all or nothing thinking?

_____

_____

_____

_____

What are some flexible thinking options?

_____

_____

_____

_____

Your friend is late for your dinner date and you are sitting alone in a restaurant.

What is the all or nothing thinking?

_____

_____

_____

_____

What are some flexible thinking options?

_____

_____

_____

_____

You have gone to the store and charged a sweater on your credit card after vowing that you wouldn't rack up anymore credit card debt.

What is the all or nothing thinking?

_____

_____

_____

_____

What are some flexible thinking options?

_____

_____

_____

_____

You have vowed not to eat any sweets for one month. After a few days in, you find yourself eating some cake at a birthday party.

What is the all or nothing thinking?

_____

_____

_____

_____

What are some flexible thinking options?

_____

_____

_____

_____

You decide to go to the gym every single day. One day, you wake up late and don't make it.

What is the all or nothing thinking?

_____

_____

_____

_____

What are some flexible thinking options?

_____

_____

_____

_____

You have decided that you can only eat 1500 calories a day. At the end of the day, you add up your calories on the Internet and find that you've eaten closer to 2000 calories.

What is the all or nothing thinking?

_____

_____

_____

_____

What are some flexible thinking options?

_____

_____

_____

_____

You get into a very big fight with your partner or spouse or a close friend. You are incredibly angry with this person.

What is the all or nothing thinking?

_____

_____

_____

_____

What are some flexible thinking options?

_____

_____

_____

_____

You have made a decision to make wholesome healthy choices and to practice good nutrition. You are at a restaurant and you order what looks like the healthiest option on the menu, fish tacos. However, when you receive your meal, you find that the fish is completely breaded and fried.

What is the all or nothing thinking?

_____

_____

_____

_____

What are some flexible thinking options?

_____

_____

_____

_____

STEP TWENTY-FOUR: Releasing Your Fear of the Binge Food

Exercise: Eating Trigger Foods without Bingeing

Refer to the exercise in step 24 of the book.

Take one item of food from its packaging and smell it. What feelings does the smell evoke? _____

_____

_____

_____

_____

Close your eyes and take one bite. Chew the food very slowly. Notice the way the food tastes on your taste buds, notice how it feels in your mouth, notice what your jaw feels like as it crunches down, notice the texture of the food and how your teeth feel chewing it.

As you concentrate on the sensation of eating, what emotions do you notice you are feeling?

_____

_____

_____

_____

What thoughts or memories are coming up for you?

_____

_____

What physical sensations are being triggered?

_____

_____

_____

_____

What emotions are you feeling?

_____

_____

_____

_____

Take another bite of the food. Chew it slowly and feel it in your mouth. Really taste it. Sense it. Tune in to your feelings. Notice what is going on in your body, your somatic response. Does your body feel excited? Tingly? Overwhelmed? Overstimulated? Shut down?

What other feelings are occurring in your body?

_____

_____

_____

_____

Think about what your reaction to the food is.

Are you triggered to eat more? _____

Do you like the taste of it? _____

What does it remind you of? _____

What does this food mean to you_____

After doing this exercise, what you notice your relationship to this binge food is?

_____

_____

_____

_____

_____

_____

_____

_____

What feelings are coming up for you as a result of doing this exercise?

_____

_____

_____

_____

_____

_____

_____

_____

STEP TWENTY-FIVE: Learning to Love Your Body

Exercise One: Body Gratitude

For each body part, write down what you feel thankful for:

Thank you toes for:_____

_____

_____

Thank you ankles for: _____

_____

_____

Thank you calves for: _____

_____

_____

Thank you knees for:_____

_____

_____

Thank you thighs for: _____

_____

_____

Thank you hips for: _____

_____

_____

Thank you belly for: _____

_____

_____

Thank you chest for: _____

_____

_____

Thank you arms for: _____

_____

_____

Thank you hands for: _____

_____

_____

Thank you face for: _____

_____

_____

Thank you nose for: _____

_____

_____

Thank you eyes for: _____

_____

_____

Thank you ears for: _____

_____

_____

Thank you head for:_____

_____

_____

Thank you body for:_____

_____

_____

Exercise Two: Letter Writing

Write a Hate Letter to the body part that you hate the most:

_____

_____

_____

_____

_____

_____

_____

_____

_____

_____

_____

_____

_____

_____

_____

_____

_____

_____

_____

_____

_____

_____

_____

_____

_____

Now, write a response to yourself from that body part:

_____

_____

_____

_____

_____

_____

_____

_____

_____

_____

_____

_____

_____

_____

_____

_____

_____

_____

_____

_____

_____

_____

_____

_____

_____

Write a note of apology for all that you've said, done, and put your body through:

_____

_____

_____

_____

_____

_____

_____

_____

_____

_____

_____

_____

_____

_____

_____

_____

_____

_____

_____

_____

_____

_____

_____

_____

_____

Write a love letter to the part of your body that you dislike the most:

_____

_____

_____

_____

_____

_____

_____

_____

_____

_____

_____

_____

_____

_____

_____

_____

_____

_____

_____

_____

_____

_____

_____

_____

_____

Exercise Three: Understanding the Impact of Body Acceptance

If I had to give up dieting, the thing about myself that I'd have to focus on would be:

_____

_____

_____

_____

_____

It would be hard for me to focus on this because:

_____

_____

_____

_____

_____

If I didn't have food or bingeing to give me comfort and solace, I am afraid that:

_____

_____

_____

_____

_____

If I decided to accept my body as it is, the negative outcome of this would be:

_____

_____

_____

_____

_____

_____

_____

_____

_____

_____

_____

_____

_____

If I decided to accept my body as it is, the positive outcome of this would be:

_____

_____

_____

_____

_____

_____

_____

_____

_____

_____

_____

_____

_____

STEP TWENTY-SEVEN: Dealing with Saboteurs

Exercise One: Identifying your Saboteurs

.Is there anyone in your life with whom you binge eat or use food with in a ritualized way? If so, who? _____

_____

_____

How does this serve or enhance your relationship? _____

_____

_____

_____

_____

What are your fears about telling this person that you no longer want food to be the center of your friendship? _____

_____

_____

_____

_____

What other things might you do that can serve a similar purpose as food did?_____

_____

_____

_____

_____

_____

_____

Can you present this to your friend in a compassionate way? If so, how?

_____

_____

_____

_____

_____

_____

Exercise Two: Identifying Systems that Perpetuate your Binge Eating

Is there anyone who would be threatened by your recovery? If so, who?

_____

What do you think would be threatening? _____

_____

_____

How can you handle it with compassion if this person tries to sabotage your

recovery?_____

_____

_____

_____

How will you take care of yourself if people become angry about you beginning to

prioritize yourself and your recovery?_____

_____

_____

Exercise Three: Creating Boundaries

Your best friend has had a horrible day. She found out that her boyfriend has been cheating on her, she got laid off, and to top it off, her mother is in the hospital. She calls you up in tears and wants you to come over for pizza and brownies and ice cream and movies. How do you handle this compassionately while still taking care of yourself? _____

_____

_____

_____

_____

_____

_____

_____

It's a Friday night and you have nothing planned. It's been a long week and you just want to stay home and take a bubble bath and relax. Your brother calls you and asks if you can come over and babysit. He and your sister-in-law would really like a much needed date night and know that you have no plans that night. How do you create boundaries and handle this compassionately while still taking care of yourself?

_____

_____

_____

_____

_____

_____

_____

_____

You are having dinner with your family and your Mom brings out a big desert that has always been a giant trigger food for you. You know that if you start in on it, you will probably spend the night (and maybe even the next several days bingeing). She knows that you've been working on recovery from binge eating and food issues. How do you gently but firmly remind her that this isn't okay and she needs to be supportive? _____

_____

_____

_____

_____

_____

_____

And what if she acts insulted or has hurt feelings? _____

_____

_____

_____

_____

It's your birthday and your girlfriends surprise you by bringing you to one of your old favorite haunts, which, incidentally is a place that has triggered binges in the past. How do you handle this situation with grace while still taking care of yourself?

_____

_____

_____

_____

_____

_____

_____

_____

You are beginning to recover and take better care of yourself, learning to say no to people, and learning how to create boundaries around food, when one of your close friends tells you that you're changing for the worse and she doesn't know that she can be your friend anymore. How do you feel about this? And how do you deal with this? _____

_____

_____

_____

_____

_____

_____

_____

_____

_____

STEP TWENTY-EIGHT: Feeling Jealous, Envious, and Making Comparisons

Exercise: Dealing with Jealousy

Are there any people who you are jealous or envious of? Who?

_____

_____

_____

_____

_____

_____

What do they have that you want?

_____

_____

_____

_____

_____

_____

How do you know that you want that?

_____

_____

_____

_____

_____

_____

How would your life be different if you had that?

_____
_____
_____
_____
_____
_____

How do you know that is true?

_____
_____
_____
_____
_____
_____

What's good and exciting about your own life?

_____
_____
_____
_____
_____
_____

What have you learned from your own struggles?

_____
_____
_____
_____
_____
_____

Are there people in the world who you had thought in the past had it all but then learned that they had their own crosses to bear? If so, who and what was the situation?

_____

_____

_____

_____

_____

_____

When you notice yourself comparing yourself to someone else, what are some ways that you can stop yourself?

_____

_____

_____

_____

_____

_____

How can you "bring it back in" when you are engaging in comparative thinking?

_____

_____

_____

_____

_____

_____

STEP THIRTY: Dealing With Desire and Wanting

Exercise One: Understanding Wants and Desires

1.Something that I desperately want is:

_____

_____

_____

_____

_____

_____

2.When I think about this, I feel:

_____

_____

_____

_____

_____

_____

3.Wanting something that I can't have makes me feel:

_____

_____

_____

_____

_____

_____

4.Think about the last time you really wanted to binge, was there something else that you were really wanting? If so, what was it?

_____

_____

_____

_____

_____

_____

6.What was going on for you when you thought about this thing that you wanted, what were you feeling?

_____

_____

_____

_____

_____

_____

7.What are some productive ways you might be supported in dealing with the pain of wanting?

_____

_____

_____

_____

_____

_____

Exercise Two: Feeling gratitude for what you do have

Name ten things that you're grateful for:

1._____

2._____

3._____

4._____

5._____

6._____

7._____

8._____

9._____

10._____

How can you bring more of these things into your life?

_____

_____

_____

_____

_____

_____

_____

_____

_____

_____

_____

_____

STEP THIRTY-ONE: What if I Relapse?

Exercise One: Understanding the Relapse

1. This relapse occurred on: _____

2. Something that had been going on around that time was:

_____

_____

_____

_____

_____

_____

3. Something that I'd been thinking a lot about on that day was:

_____

_____

_____

_____

_____

_____

4. I was feeling this way on that day:

_____

_____

_____

_____

_____

_____

5. Aside from bingeing, what else could I have done to help me find some peace on that day, even to find peace around the anxiety of bingeing?

_____

_____

_____

_____

_____

_____

6. In the future, what warning signs will I have that a relapse is imminent?

_____

_____

_____

_____

_____

_____

7.What kind of plans and precautions can I take when those triggering times arise?

_____

_____

_____

_____

_____

_____

Exercise Two: Step-by-Step Behavioral Chain Analysis

1. Describe the binge. Where did it happen? What time did it happen? What did you binge on? Was anyone else around? How much did you eat?

_____

_____

_____

_____

_____

_____

2. What were you feeling while you were bingeing?

_____

_____

_____

_____

_____

3. How intense was the binge compared to other binges that you've had? Was it more intense, less intense? How did it compare?

_____

_____

_____

_____

_____

4.Was there a particular event that you can point to that triggered the binge?

_____

_____

_____

_____

_____

_____

5. What happened just before the binge?

_____

_____

_____

_____

_____

_____

6. What happened an hour before the binge?

_____

_____

_____

_____

_____

_____

7. What happened earlier that day?

_____

_____

_____

_____

_____

_____

8. How were you feeling that day?

_____

_____

_____

_____

_____

_____

9. Did you try anything to prevent the binge?

_____

_____

_____

_____

_____

_____

10. What, if any physical triggers were you feeling? (for example: did you eat a trigger food, or did you smell or pass a trigger food, were you very hungry, were you in any physical pain? had you been restricting?)

_____

_____

_____

_____

_____

_____

11. Can you pinpoint when the binge sequence began?

_____

_____

_____

_____

_____

_____

12. What was going on for you emotionally the moment the sequence began? What were you doing, thinking, feeling, imagining at that time?

_____

_____

_____

_____

_____

_____

13. Was there anything that happened the day before that led into this day?

_____

_____

_____

_____

_____

_____

14. How was the day before or the last day that you did not binge different from this day?

_____

_____

_____

_____

_____

_____

15. What kind of *vulnerability factors* were involved with the binge, what made you more vulnerable to each link in the chain that led up to the binge? If you are unsure, the following four questions can help you answer that.

_____

_____

_____

_____

_____

_____

16.Were there physical factors such as pain or illness, hunger, fullness, lack of sleep, fatigue, or an injury, were there drugs or alcohol involved?

_____

_____

_____

_____

_____

_____

17. Was there some kind of external trigger such as a stressful event, stressful news, an argument or confrontation with someone?

_____

_____

_____

_____

_____

_____

18. Were you reacting to something that you learned either positive or negative?

_____

_____

_____

_____

_____

_____

19. Did you have some kind of challenging emotion like anger, jealousy, sadness, fear, or loneliness?

_____

_____

_____

_____

_____

_____

20.Were there previous behaviors that you acted out that triggered, stressed and built on this chain? For example, snacking on a food that you did not want to eat during a time when you were not hungry.

_____

_____

_____

_____

_____

_____

21. How did that link lead to the next link, which led to the next link, which eventually became the binge?

_____

_____

_____

_____

_____

_____

22.Link by link, describe how the chain of events led up to the binge.

_____

_____

_____

_____

_____

_____

23. Looking back at each link, what thoughts, feelings, or beliefs did you have during and after each behavior?

_____

_____

_____

_____

_____

_____

24. Thinking about his objectively, as if you directing someone other than yourself, what different links could you have injected into the sequence that could have created a more positive outcome?

_____

_____

_____

_____

_____

_____

25. Was there a solution at the end of any one of these links? Was bingeing a solution?

_____

_____

_____

_____

_____

_____

26. Did bingeing help at all? If so, how?

_____

_____

_____

_____

_____

_____

27. How could you have avoided bingeing?

_____

_____

_____

_____

_____

_____

28. Understanding what you know now about what you did, how could you prevent this in the future?

_____

_____

_____

_____

_____

_____

STEP THIRTY-TWO: Understanding How Your Family Dynamics Have Influenced Your Binge Eating

Exercise: How has your family contributed to your eating disorder?

1.The following people commented on my body or eating habits:

_____

_____

_____

_____

_____

_____

2.What kinds of things did they say?

_____

_____

_____

_____

_____

_____

3.What kinds of beliefs did this lead you to have about your body?

_____

_____

_____

_____

_____

_____

4.What kinds of beliefs this lead you to have about your own sense of worth?

_____

_____

_____

_____

_____

_____

5.When you think about this now, what do you feel?

_____

_____

_____

_____

_____

_____

6.How did your family discuss feelings?

_____

_____

_____

_____

_____

_____

7.What did you learn from this?

_____

_____

_____

_____

_____

_____

8. Is there a different way that you wish your family could have dealt with feelings?

_____

_____

_____

_____

_____

_____

9. If you could change something now about the way you acknowledge and discuss feelings, how would you do that?

_____

_____

_____

_____

_____

_____

10. When do you first remember having body image issues?

_____

_____

_____

_____

_____

_____

11. Did you tell anyone about it? How did they react?

_____

_____

_____

_____

_____

_____

12. When do you first remember dieting?

_____

_____

_____

_____

_____

_____

13. When do you first remember bingeing?

_____

_____

_____

_____

_____

_____

14. Was there anyone in your family who engaged in any kind of eating disordered behavior, for example: bingeing, obsessive dieting, food obsession, bulimia, compulsive behaviors around food, food hoarding, food restricting, anorexia, compulsive exercise, body image issues? If so, who?

_____

_____

_____

_____

_____

_____

15. What was that like for you? What did you think about it? How did it affect you when you were younger?

_____

_____

_____

_____

_____

_____

16. What did you learn from watching this behavior and how has it shaped your current beliefs?

_____

_____

_____

_____

_____

_____

17. If you could change your core beliefs and behavior, what would you change them to?

_____

_____

_____

_____

_____

_____

_____

_____

_____

_____

_____

STEP THIRTY-FOUR: Tell Your Story

You can use the following prompts to write your story, or just write it on your own-

The first time I remember thinking about food or my body...

_____

_____

_____

_____

_____

_____

_____

_____

_____

_____

_____

Meals in my family were like this...

_____

_____

_____

_____

_____

_____

_____

_____

_____

Food in my family was like this...

_____
_____
_____
_____
_____
_____
_____
_____
_____
_____

Body image in my family was like this...

_____
_____
_____
_____
_____
_____
_____
_____
_____
_____
_____
_____
_____

The first time I binged:

_____

_____

_____

_____

_____

_____

I used to binge when:

_____

_____

_____

_____

_____

_____

My bingeing then evolved into:

_____

_____

_____

_____

_____

I used food to:

_____

_____

_____

_____

_____

_____

I decided to start in recovery because:

_____

_____

_____

_____

_____

_____

This is how it's been going:

_____

_____

_____

_____

_____

_____

_____

_____

_____

_____

_____

_____

_____

_____

_____

_____

_____

_____

Write your own story:

Hunger and Satiety Scale

0	Starvation mode. Void of feelings. No energy, tired, empty.
1	Ravenous. Feeling uncomfortably hungry. Dizzy, grumpy.
2	Very Hungry, unable to focus on work or conversation.
3	Hungry. Stomach is beginning to growl, you are beginning to lose focus.
4	Getting Hungry. First thoughts of food begin.
5	Neutral. Not hungry, not full. Not obsessing about food. Nurtured, productive, able to focus. If you are eating, you can still eat more.
6	Satisfied. You've eaten enough to be content. You are not uncomfortable, yet you do not need more.
7	Slightly Full. A bit more than satisfied. You might feel like you had a bit too much.
8	Very Full. You begin to feel bloated as though you've had too much.
9	Uncomfortably full. You just want to go to sleep. You might feel depressed or regretful.
10	Completely Stuffed. You feel like you might throw up. You are in pain, you can't focus, and you don't know how you got here.

Red- Danger Zone

Green- Go ahead and Eat

Yellow- Slow down, you can stop eating now

Alternative Action Log

Trigger: What Kind of Trigger was this, emotional, physical or situational?

_____
_____
_____
_____
_____

Describe What Happened:

_____
_____
_____
_____
_____

Feelings: (What am I feeling about it?)

_____
_____
_____
_____

Short Term Solution: (What do I want to do in the short term to make me feel better?)

_____
_____
_____
_____

Long Term Consequence: (How Will that make me feel later, or tomorrow?)

_____
_____
_____
_____

Alternative Behavior: (What else can I do to make myself feel better?)

_____
_____
_____
_____

Alternative Action Log

Trigger: What Kind of Trigger was this, emotional, physical or situational?

_____
_____
_____
_____
_____

Describe What Happened:

_____
_____
_____
_____
_____

Feelings: (What am I feeling about it?)

_____
_____
_____
_____

Short Term Solution: (What do I want to do in the short term to make me feel better?)

_____
_____
_____
_____

Long Term Consequence: (How Will that make me feel later, or tomorrow?)

_____
_____
_____

Alternative Behavior: (What else can I do to make myself feel better?)

_____
_____
_____
_____

Alternative Action Log

Trigger: What Kind of Trigger was this, emotional, physical or situational?

_____

_____

_____

_____

_____

Describe What Happened:

_____

_____

_____

_____

_____

Feelings: (What am I feeling about it?)

_____

_____

_____

_____

Short Term Solution: (What do I want to do in the short term to make me feel better?)

_____

_____

_____

_____

Long Term Consequence: (How Will that make me feel later, or tomorrow?)

_____

_____

_____

_____

Alternative Behavior: (What else can I do to make myself feel better?)

_____

_____

_____

_____

Alternative Action Log

Trigger: What Kind of Trigger was this, emotional, physical or situational?

_____
_____
_____
_____
_____

Describe What Happened:

_____
_____
_____
_____
_____

Feelings: (What am I feeling about it?)

_____
_____
_____
_____

Short Term Solution: (What do I want to do in the short term to make me feel better?)

_____
_____
_____
_____

Long Term Consequence: (How Will that make me feel later, or tomorrow?)

_____
_____
_____

Alternative Behavior: (What else can I do to make myself feel better?)

_____
_____
_____
_____

Alternative Action Log

Trigger: What Kind of Trigger was this, emotional, physical or situational?

_____
_____
_____
_____
_____

Describe What Happened:

_____
_____
_____
_____
_____

Feelings: (What am I feeling about it?)

_____
_____
_____
_____

Short Term Solution: (What do I want to do in the short term to make me feel better?)

_____
_____
_____
_____

Long Term Consequence: (How Will that make me feel later, or tomorrow?)

_____
_____
_____
_____

Alternative Behavior: (What else can I do to make myself feel better?)

_____
_____
_____
_____

Alternative Action Log

Trigger: What Kind of Trigger was this, emotional, physical or situational?

_____
_____
_____
_____
_____

Describe What Happened:

_____
_____
_____
_____
_____

Feelings: (What am I feeling about it?)

_____
_____
_____
_____

Short Term Solution: (What do I want to do in the short term to make me feel better?)

_____
_____
_____
_____

Long Term Consequence: (How Will that make me feel later, or tomorrow?)

_____
_____
_____
_____

Alternative Behavior: (What else can I do to make myself feel better?)

_____
_____
_____
_____

Alternative Action Log

Trigger: What Kind of Trigger was this, emotional, physical or situational?

_____
_____
_____
_____
_____

Describe What Happened:

_____
_____
_____
_____
_____

Feelings: (What am I feeling about it?)

_____
_____
_____
_____

Short Term Solution: (What do I want to do in the short term to make me feel better?)

_____
_____
_____
_____

Long Term Consequence: (How Will that make me feel later, or tomorrow?)

_____
_____
_____
_____

Alternative Behavior: (What else can I do to make myself feel better?)

_____
_____
_____
_____

Alternative Action Log

Trigger: What Kind of Trigger was this, emotional, physical or situational?

_____
_____
_____
_____
_____

Describe What Happened:

_____
_____
_____
_____
_____

Feelings: (What am I feeling about it?)

_____
_____
_____
_____

Short Term Solution: (What do I want to do in the short term to make me feel better?)

_____
_____
_____
_____

Long Term Consequence: (How Will that make me feel later, or tomorrow?)

_____
_____
_____
_____

Alternative Behavior: (What else can I do to make myself feel better?)

_____
_____
_____
_____

Alternative Action Log

Trigger: What Kind of Trigger was this, emotional, physical or situational?

_____
_____
_____
_____
_____

Describe What Happened:

_____
_____
_____
_____
_____

Feelings: (What am I feeling about it?)

_____
_____
_____
_____

Short Term Solution: (What do I want to do in the short term to make me feel better?)

_____
_____
_____
_____

Long Term Consequence: (How Will that make me feel later, or tomorrow?)

_____
_____
_____
_____

Alternative Behavior: (What else can I do to make myself feel better?)

_____
_____
_____
_____

Alternative Action Log

Trigger: What Kind of Trigger was this, emotional, physical or situational?

_____
_____
_____
_____
_____

Describe What Happened:

_____
_____
_____
_____
_____

Feelings: (What am I feeling about it?)

_____
_____
_____
_____

Short Term Solution: (What do I want to do in the short term to make me feel better?)

_____
_____
_____
_____

Long Term Consequence: (How Will that make me feel later, or tomorrow?)

_____
_____
_____
_____

Alternative Behavior: (What else can I do to make myself feel better?)

_____
_____
_____
_____

Food and Mood Log

HOW DO YOU FEEL PHYSICALLY BEFORE EATING?

_____
_____
_____

HOW DO YOU FEEL EMOTIONALLY BEFORE EATING?

_____
_____
_____

DESCRIBE YOUR LEVEL OF HUNGER BEFORE EATING –USE H/S SCALE

_____
_____
_____

DESCRIBE WHAT YOU ATE INCLUDING SERVING SIZE:

_____
_____
_____
_____

HOW DO YOU FEEL PHYSICALLY AFTER EATING?

_____
_____
_____

HOW DO YOU FEEL EMOTIONALLY AFTER EATING?

_____
_____
_____
_____

DESCRIBE YOUR LEVEL OF HUNGER AFTER EATING:

_____
_____
_____
_____

Food and Mood Log

HOW DO YOU FEEL PHYSICALLY BEFORE EATING?

_____
_____
_____

HOW DO YOU FEEL EMOTIONALLY BEFORE EATING?

_____
_____
_____

DESCRIBE YOUR LEVEL OF HUNGER BEFORE EATING –USE H/S SCALE

_____
_____
_____

DESCRIBE WHAT YOU ATE INCLUDING SERVING SIZE:

_____
_____
_____
_____

HOW DO YOU FEEL PHYSICALLY AFTER EATING?

_____
_____
_____

HOW DO YOU FEEL EMOTIONALLY AFTER EATING?

_____
_____
_____
_____

DESCRIBE YOUR LEVEL OF HUNGER AFTER EATING:

_____
_____
_____
_____

Food and Mood Log

HOW DO YOU FEEL PHYSICALLY BEFORE EATING?

_____
_____
_____

HOW DO YOU FEEL EMOTIONALLY BEFORE EATING?

_____
_____
_____

DESCRIBE YOUR LEVEL OF HUNGER BEFORE EATING –USE H/S SCALE

_____
_____
_____

DESCRIBE WHAT YOU ATE INCLUDING SERVING SIZE:

_____
_____
_____
_____

HOW DO YOU FEEL PHYSICALLY AFTER EATING?

_____
_____
_____

HOW DO YOU FEEL EMOTIONALLY AFTER EATING?

_____
_____
_____
_____

DESCRIBE YOUR LEVEL OF HUNGER AFTER EATING:

_____
_____
_____
_____

Food and Mood Log

HOW DO YOU FEEL PHYSICALLY BEFORE EATING?

_____
_____
_____

HOW DO YOU FEEL EMOTIONALLY BEFORE EATING?

_____
_____
_____

DESCRIBE YOUR LEVEL OF HUNGER BEFORE EATING –USE H/S SCALE

_____
_____
_____

DESCRIBE WHAT YOU ATE INCLUDING SERVING SIZE:

_____
_____
_____
_____

HOW DO YOU FEEL PHYSICALLY AFTER EATING?

_____
_____
_____

HOW DO YOU FEEL EMOTIONALLY AFTER EATING?

_____
_____
_____
_____

DESCRIBE YOUR LEVEL OF HUNGER AFTER EATING:

_____
_____
_____
_____

Food and Mood Log

HOW DO YOU FEEL PHYSICALLY BEFORE EATING?

_____
_____
_____

HOW DO YOU FEEL EMOTIONALLY BEFORE EATING?

_____
_____
_____

DESCRIBE YOUR LEVEL OF HUNGER BEFORE EATING –USE H/S SCALE

_____
_____
_____

DESCRIBE WHAT YOU ATE INCLUDING SERVING SIZE:

_____
_____
_____
_____

HOW DO YOU FEEL PHYSICALLY AFTER EATING?

_____
_____
_____

HOW DO YOU FEEL EMOTIONALLY AFTER EATING?

_____
_____
_____

DESCRIBE YOUR LEVEL OF HUNGER AFTER EATING:

_____
_____
_____
_____

Food and Mood Log

HOW DO YOU FEEL PHYSICALLY BEFORE EATING?

_____
_____
_____

HOW DO YOU FEEL EMOTIONALLY BEFORE EATING?

_____
_____
_____

DESCRIBE YOUR LEVEL OF HUNGER BEFORE EATING –USE H/S SCALE

_____
_____
_____

DESCRIBE WHAT YOU ATE INCLUDING SERVING SIZE:

_____
_____
_____
_____

HOW DO YOU FEEL PHYSICALLY AFTER EATING?

_____
_____
_____

HOW DO YOU FEEL EMOTIONALLY AFTER EATING?

_____
_____
_____
_____

DESCRIBE YOUR LEVEL OF HUNGER AFTER EATING:

_____
_____
_____
_____

Food and Mood Log

HOW DO YOU FEEL PHYSICALLY BEFORE EATING?

_____
_____
_____

HOW DO YOU FEEL EMOTIONALLY BEFORE EATING?

_____
_____
_____

DESCRIBE YOUR LEVEL OF HUNGER BEFORE EATING –USE H/S SCALE

_____
_____
_____

DESCRIBE WHAT YOU ATE INCLUDING SERVING SIZE:

_____
_____
_____
_____

HOW DO YOU FEEL PHYSICALLY AFTER EATING?

_____
_____
_____

HOW DO YOU FEEL EMOTIONALLY AFTER EATING?

_____
_____
_____
_____

DESCRIBE YOUR LEVEL OF HUNGER AFTER EATING:

_____
_____
_____
_____

Food and Mood Log

HOW DO YOU FEEL PHYSICALLY BEFORE EATING?

_____
_____
_____

HOW DO YOU FEEL EMOTIONALLY BEFORE EATING?

_____
_____
_____

DESCRIBE YOUR LEVEL OF HUNGER BEFORE EATING –USE H/S SCALE

_____
_____
_____

DESCRIBE WHAT YOU ATE INCLUDING SERVING SIZE:

_____
_____
_____
_____

HOW DO YOU FEEL PHYSICALLY AFTER EATING?

_____
_____
_____

HOW DO YOU FEEL EMOTIONALLY AFTER EATING?

_____
_____
_____
_____

DESCRIBE YOUR LEVEL OF HUNGER AFTER EATING:

_____
_____
_____
_____

Food and Mood Log

HOW DO YOU FEEL PHYSICALLY BEFORE EATING?

_____
_____
_____

HOW DO YOU FEEL EMOTIONALLY BEFORE EATING?

_____
_____
_____

DESCRIBE YOUR LEVEL OF HUNGER BEFORE EATING –USE H/S SCALE

_____
_____
_____

DESCRIBE WHAT YOU ATE INCLUDING SERVING SIZE:

_____
_____
_____
_____

HOW DO YOU FEEL PHYSICALLY AFTER EATING?

_____
_____
_____

HOW DO YOU FEEL EMOTIONALLY AFTER EATING?

_____
_____
_____
_____

DESCRIBE YOUR LEVEL OF HUNGER AFTER EATING:

_____
_____
_____
_____

Food and Mood Log

HOW DO YOU FEEL PHYSICALLY BEFORE EATING?

_____
_____
_____

HOW DO YOU FEEL EMOTIONALLY BEFORE EATING?

_____
_____
_____

DESCRIBE YOUR LEVEL OF HUNGER BEFORE EATING –USE H/S SCALE

_____
_____
_____

DESCRIBE WHAT YOU ATE INCLUDING SERVING SIZE:

_____
_____
_____
_____

HOW DO YOU FEEL PHYSICALLY AFTER EATING?

_____
_____
_____

HOW DO YOU FEEL EMOTIONALLY AFTER EATING?

_____
_____
_____
_____

DESCRIBE YOUR LEVEL OF HUNGER AFTER EATING:

_____
_____
_____
_____

Meal Planner

Meal: Time: Place: Planned Food:

_____   _____   _____   _____

_____   _____   _____   _____

_____   _____   _____   _____

_____   _____   _____   _____

_____   _____   _____   _____

_____   _____   _____   _____

_____   _____   _____   _____

_____   _____   _____   _____

_____   _____   _____   _____

_____   _____   _____   _____

_____   _____   _____   _____

_____   _____   _____   _____

_____   _____   _____   _____

_____   _____   _____   _____

_____   _____   _____   _____

_____   _____   _____   _____

_____   _____   _____   _____

Meal Planner

Meal: Time: Place: Planned Food:

_____   _____   _____   _____

_____   _____   _____   _____

_____   _____   _____   _____

_____   _____   _____   _____

_____   _____   _____   _____

_____   _____   _____   _____

_____   _____   _____   _____

_____   _____   _____   _____

_____   _____   _____   _____

_____   _____   _____   _____

_____   _____   _____   _____

_____   _____   _____   _____

_____   _____   _____   _____

_____   _____   _____   _____

_____   _____   _____   _____

_____   _____   _____   _____

_____   _____   _____   _____

_____   _____   _____   _____

_____   _____   _____   _____

_____   _____   _____   _____

Meal Planner

Meal: Time: Place: Planned Food:

_____   _____   _____   _____

_____   _____   _____   _____

_____   _____   _____   _____

_____   _____   _____   _____

_____   _____   _____   _____

_____   _____   _____   _____

_____   _____   _____   _____

_____   _____   _____   _____

_____   _____   _____   _____

_____   _____   _____   _____

_____   _____   _____   _____

_____   _____   _____   _____

_____   _____   _____   _____

_____   _____   _____   _____

_____   _____   _____   _____

_____   _____   _____   _____

_____   _____   _____   _____

_____   _____   _____   _____

_____   _____   _____   _____

Meal Planner

Meal: Time: Place: Planned Food:

Meal Planner

Meal: Time: Place: Planned Food:

_____   _____   _____   _____

_____   _____   _____   _____

_____   _____   _____   _____

_____   _____   _____   _____

_____   _____   _____   _____

_____   _____   _____   _____

_____   _____   _____   _____

_____   _____   _____   _____

_____   _____   _____   _____

_____   _____   _____   _____

_____   _____   _____   _____

_____   _____   _____   _____

_____   _____   _____   _____

_____   _____   _____   _____

_____   _____   _____   _____

_____   _____   _____   _____

_____   _____   _____   _____

_____   _____   _____   _____

Meal Planner

Meal:	Time:	Place:	Planned Food:
_____	_____	_____	_____
_____	_____	_____	_____
_____	_____	_____	_____
_____	_____	_____	_____
_____	_____	_____	_____
_____	_____	_____	_____
_____	_____	_____	_____
_____	_____	_____	_____
_____	_____	_____	_____
_____	_____	_____	_____
_____	_____	_____	_____
_____	_____	_____	_____
_____	_____	_____	_____
_____	_____	_____	_____
_____	_____	_____	_____
_____	_____	_____	_____
_____	_____	_____	_____
_____	_____	_____	_____
_____	_____	_____	_____

Meal Planner

Meal: Time: Place: Planned Food:

Meal:	Time:	Place:	Planned Food:

Meal Planner

Meal:	Time:	Place:	Planned Food:
_____	_____	_____	_____
_____	_____	_____	_____
_____	_____	_____	_____
_____	_____	_____	_____
_____	_____	_____	_____
_____	_____	_____	_____
_____	_____	_____	_____
_____	_____	_____	_____
_____	_____	_____	_____
_____	_____	_____	_____
_____	_____	_____	_____
_____	_____	_____	_____
_____	_____	_____	_____
_____	_____	_____	_____
_____	_____	_____	_____
_____	_____	_____	_____
_____	_____	_____	_____
_____	_____	_____	_____
_____	_____	_____	_____
_____	_____	_____	_____

Meal Planner

Meal: Time: Place: Planned Food:

_____   _____   _____   _____

_____   _____   _____   _____

_____   _____   _____   _____

_____   _____   _____   _____

_____   _____   _____   _____

_____   _____   _____   _____

_____   _____   _____   _____

_____   _____   _____   _____

_____   _____   _____   _____

_____   _____   _____   _____

_____   _____   _____   _____

_____   _____   _____   _____

_____   _____   _____   _____

_____   _____   _____   _____

_____   _____   _____   _____

_____   _____   _____   _____

_____   _____   _____   _____

_____   _____   _____   _____

_____   _____   _____   _____

Meal Planner

Meal:	Time:	Place:	Planned Food:
_____	_____	_____	_____
_____	_____	_____	_____
_____	_____	_____	_____
_____	_____	_____	_____
_____	_____	_____	_____
_____	_____	_____	_____
_____	_____	_____	_____
_____	_____	_____	_____
_____	_____	_____	_____
_____	_____	_____	_____
_____	_____	_____	_____
_____	_____	_____	_____
_____	_____	_____	_____
_____	_____	_____	_____
_____	_____	_____	_____
_____	_____	_____	_____
_____	_____	_____	_____
_____	_____	_____	_____
_____	_____	_____	_____

Meal Planner

Meal: Time: Place: Planned Food:

_____ _____ _____ _____

_____ _____ _____ _____

_____ _____ _____ _____

_____ _____ _____ _____

_____ _____ _____ _____

_____ _____ _____ _____

_____ _____ _____ _____

_____ _____ _____ _____

_____ _____ _____ _____

_____ _____ _____ _____

_____ _____ _____ _____

_____ _____ _____ _____

_____ _____ _____ _____

_____ _____ _____ _____

_____ _____ _____ _____

_____ _____ _____ _____

_____ _____ _____ _____

_____ _____ _____ _____

_____ _____ _____ _____

_____ _____ _____ _____

217

Meal Planner

Meal:　　　　　　Time:　　　　　　Place:　　　　　　Planned Food:

———————————　　———————————　　————————————　　————————————

———————————　　———————————　　————————————　　————————————

———————————　　———————————　　————————————　　————————————

———————————　　———————————　　————————————　　————————————

———————————　　———————————　　————————————　　————————————

———————————　　———————————　　————————————　　————————————

———————————　　———————————　　————————————　　————————————

———————————　　———————————　　————————————　　————————————

———————————　　———————————　　————————————　　————————————

———————————　　———————————　　————————————　　————————————

———————————　　———————————　　————————————　　————————————

———————————　　———————————　　————————————　　————————————

———————————　　———————————　　————————————　　————————————

———————————　　———————————　　————————————　　————————————

———————————　　———————————　　————————————　　————————————

———————————　　———————————　　————————————　　————————————

———————————　　———————————　　————————————　　————————————

———————————　　———————————　　————————————　　————————————

———————————　　———————————　　————————————　　————————————

Procrastination Worksheet

1. What is it that you are yourself procrastinating on?

_____

_____

2. How do you feel about this particular task?

_____

_____

_____

_____

3. How do you feel while you are doing this task?

_____

_____

_____

_____

4. How do you feel while you're thinking about this task?

_____

_____

_____

5. How does food help you when you are procrastinating?

_____

_____

_____

_____

6. What are your fears about doing this task?

_____

_____

_____

_____

7. What are your fears about not doing this task?

_____

_____

_____

_____

Procrastination Worksheet

1. What is it that you are yourself procrastinating on?

_____

_____

2. How do you feel about this particular task?

_____

_____

_____

_____

3. How do you feel while you are doing this task?

_____

_____

_____

_____

4. How do you feel while you're thinking about this task?

_____

_____

_____

5. How does food help you when you are procrastinating?

_____

_____

_____

_____

6. What are your fears about doing this task?

_____

_____

_____

_____

7. What are your fears about not doing this task?

_____

_____

_____

_____

Procrastination Worksheet

1. What is it that you are yourself procrastinating on?

_____

_____

2. How do you feel about this particular task?

_____

_____

_____

_____

3. How do you feel while you are doing this task?

_____

_____

_____

_____

4. How do you feel while you're thinking about this task?

_____

_____

_____

5. How does food help you when you are procrastinating?

_____

_____

_____

_____

6. What are your fears about doing this task?

_____

_____

_____

_____

7. What are your fears about not doing this task?

_____

_____

_____

_____

Procrastination Worksheet

1. What is it that you are yourself procrastinating on?

_____

_____

2. How do you feel about this particular task?

_____

_____

_____

_____

3. How do you feel while you are doing this task?

_____

_____

_____

_____

4. How do you feel while you're thinking about this task?

_____

_____

_____

5. How does food help you when you are procrastinating?

_____

_____

_____

_____

6. What are your fears about doing this task?

_____

_____

_____

_____

7. What are your fears about not doing this task?

_____

_____

_____

_____

Procrastination Worksheet

1. What is it that you are yourself procrastinating on?

_____

_____

2. How do you feel about this particular task?

_____

_____

_____

_____

3. How do you feel while you are doing this task?

_____

_____

_____

_____

4. How do you feel while you're thinking about this task?

_____

_____

_____

5. How does food help you when you are procrastinating?

_____

_____

_____

_____

6. What are your fears about doing this task?

_____

_____

_____

_____

7. What are your fears about not doing this task?

_____

_____

_____

_____

Procrastination Worksheet

1. What is it that you are yourself procrastinating on?

_____

_____

2. How do you feel about this particular task?

_____

_____

_____

_____

3. How do you feel while you are doing this task?

_____

_____

_____

_____

4. How do you feel while you're thinking about this task?

_____

_____

_____

5. How does food help you when you are procrastinating?

_____

_____

_____

_____

6. What are your fears about doing this task?

_____

_____

_____

_____

7. What are your fears about not doing this task?

_____

_____

_____

_____

Procrastination Worksheet

1. What is it that you are yourself procrastinating on?
_____
_____

2. How do you feel about this particular task?
_____
_____
_____
_____

3. How do you feel while you are doing this task?
_____
_____
_____
_____

4. How do you feel while you're thinking about this task?
_____
_____
_____

5. How does food help you when you are procrastinating?
_____
_____
_____
_____

6. What are your fears about doing this task?
_____
_____
_____
_____

7. What are your fears about not doing this task?
_____
_____
_____
_____

Procrastination Worksheet

1. What is it that you are yourself procrastinating on?

_____

_____

2. How do you feel about this particular task?

_____

_____

_____

_____

3. How do you feel while you are doing this task?

_____

_____

_____

_____

4. How do you feel while you're thinking about this task?

_____

_____

_____

5. How does food help you when you are procrastinating?

_____

_____

_____

_____

6. What are your fears about doing this task?

_____

_____

_____

_____

7. What are your fears about not doing this task?

_____

_____

_____

_____

Procrastination Worksheet

1. What is it that you are yourself procrastinating on?

_____

_____

2. How do you feel about this particular task?

_____

_____

_____

_____

3. How do you feel while you are doing this task?

_____

_____

_____

_____

4. How do you feel while you're thinking about this task?

_____

_____

_____

5. How does food help you when you are procrastinating?

_____

_____

_____

_____

6. What are your fears about doing this task?

_____

_____

_____

_____

7. What are your fears about not doing this task?

_____

_____

_____

_____

Procrastination Worksheet

1. What is it that you are yourself procrastinating on?

_____

_____

2. How do you feel about this particular task?

_____

_____

_____

_____

3. How do you feel while you are doing this task?

_____

_____

_____

_____

4. How do you feel while you're thinking about this task?

_____

_____

_____

5. How does food help you when you are procrastinating?

_____

_____

_____

_____

6. What are your fears about doing this task?

_____

_____

_____

_____

7. What are your fears about not doing this task?

_____

_____

_____

_____

Procrastination Worksheet

1. What is it that you are yourself procrastinating on?

_____

_____

2. How do you feel about this particular task?

_____

_____

_____

_____

3. How do you feel while you are doing this task?

_____

_____

_____

_____

4. How do you feel while you're thinking about this task?

_____

_____

_____

5. How does food help you when you are procrastinating?

_____

_____

_____

_____

6. What are your fears about doing this task?

_____

_____

_____

_____

7. What are your fears about not doing this task?

_____

_____

_____

_____

Procrastination Worksheet

1. What is it that you are yourself procrastinating on?

_____

_____

2. How do you feel about this particular task?

_____

_____

_____

_____

3. How do you feel while you are doing this task?

_____

_____

_____

_____

4. How do you feel while you're thinking about this task?

_____

_____

_____

5. How does food help you when you are procrastinating?

_____

_____

_____

_____

6. What are your fears about doing this task?

_____

_____

_____

_____

7. What are your fears about not doing this task?

_____

_____

_____

_____

Before Bed Journal

I think:_____

_____

_____

_____

_____

I need: _____

_____

_____

_____

_____

I feel: _____

_____

_____

_____

_____

_____

_____

Today I:_____

_____

_____

_____

_____

I wish that:_____

_____

_____

_____

_____

The worst part of my day today was: _____

_____

_____

The best part of my day today was: _____

_____

_____

Anything Else I need to sort through: _____

_____

_____

_____

_____

_____

_____

_____

_____

_____

_____

_____

_____

_____

_____

_____

_____

_____

_____

_____

_____

_____

_____

_____

_____

_____

_____

_____

_____

_____

_____

_____

_____

_____

_____

_____

_____

_____

Before Bed Journal

I think:_____

_____

_____

_____

_____

I need: _____

_____

_____

_____

_____

I feel: _____

_____

_____

_____

_____

_____

_____

Today I:_____

_____

_____

_____

_____

I wish that:_____

_____

_____

_____

_____

_____

The worst part of my day today was: _____

_____

_____

The best part of my day today was: _____

_____

_____

Anything Else I need to sort through: _____

_____
_____
_____
_____
_____
_____
_____
_____
_____
_____
_____
_____
_____
_____
_____
_____
_____
_____
_____
_____
_____
_____
_____
_____
_____
_____
_____
_____
_____
_____
_____
_____
_____
_____
_____
_____
_____
_____
_____

Before Bed Journal

I think:_____
_____
_____
_____
_____

I need: _____
_____
_____
_____
_____

I feel: _____
_____
_____
_____
_____
_____
_____

Today I:_____
_____
_____
_____
_____

I wish that:_____
_____
_____
_____
_____

The worst part of my day today was: _____
_____
_____
_____

The best part of my day today was: _____
_____
_____
_____

Anything Else I need to sort through: _____

_____
_____
_____
_____
_____
_____
_____
_____
_____
_____
_____
_____
_____
_____
_____
_____
_____
_____
_____
_____
_____
_____
_____
_____
_____
_____
_____
_____
_____
_____
_____
_____
_____
_____
_____
_____
_____
_____
_____

Before Bed Journal

I think:_____
_____
_____
_____
_____

I need: _____
_____
_____
_____
_____

I feel: _____
_____
_____
_____
_____
_____
_____

Today I:_____
_____
_____
_____
_____

I wish that:_____
_____
_____
_____
_____

The worst part of my day today was: _____
_____
_____

The best part of my day today was: _____
_____
_____
_____

Anything Else I need to sort through: _____

_____
_____
_____
_____
_____
_____
_____
_____
_____
_____
_____
_____
_____
_____
_____
_____
_____
_____
_____
_____
_____
_____
_____
_____
_____
_____
_____
_____
_____
_____
_____
_____
_____
_____
_____
_____

Before Bed Journal

I think:_____

_____

_____

_____

_____

I need: _____

_____

_____

_____

_____

I feel: _____

_____

_____

_____

_____

_____

_____

Today I:_____

_____

_____

_____

_____

I wish that:_____

_____

_____

_____

_____

The worst part of my day today was: _____

_____

_____

The best part of my day today was: _____

_____

_____

Anything Else I need to sort through: _____
_____
_____
_____
_____
_____
_____
_____
_____
_____
_____
_____
_____
_____
_____
_____
_____
_____
_____
_____
_____
_____
_____
_____
_____
_____
_____
_____
_____
_____
_____
_____
_____
_____
_____
_____
_____
_____
_____

Before Bed Journal

I think:_____
_____
_____
_____
_____

I need: _____
_____
_____
_____
_____

I feel: _____
_____
_____
_____
_____
_____
_____

Today I:_____
_____
_____
_____

I wish that:_____
_____
_____
_____
_____

The worst part of my day today was: _____
_____
_____

The best part of my day today was: _____
_____
_____
_____

Anything Else I need to sort through: _____
_____
_____
_____
_____
_____
_____
_____
_____
_____
_____
_____
_____
_____
_____
_____
_____
_____
_____
_____
_____
_____
_____
_____
_____
_____
_____
_____
_____
_____
_____
_____
_____
_____
_____
_____
_____
_____

Before Bed Journal

I think:_____
_____
_____
_____
_____

I need: _____
_____
_____
_____
_____

I feel: _____
_____
_____
_____
_____
_____
_____

Today I:_____
_____
_____
_____
_____

I wish that:_____
_____
_____
_____
_____

The worst part of my day today was: _____
_____
_____
_____

The best part of my day today was: _____
_____
_____
_____

Anything Else I need to sort through: _____

_____

_____

_____

_____

_____

_____

_____

_____

_____

_____

_____

_____

_____

_____

_____

_____

_____

_____

_____

_____

_____

_____

_____

_____

_____

_____

_____

_____

_____

_____

_____

_____

_____

_____

_____

_____

_____

_____

_____

_____

Before Bed Journal

I think:_____
_____
_____
_____
_____

I need: _____
_____
_____
_____
_____

I feel: _____
_____
_____
_____
_____
_____
_____

Today I:_____
_____
_____
_____
_____

I wish that:_____
_____
_____
_____
_____

The worst part of my day today was: _____
_____
_____

The best part of my day today was: _____
_____
_____

Anything Else I need to sort through: _____

_____
_____
_____
_____
_____
_____
_____
_____
_____
_____
_____
_____
_____
_____
_____
_____
_____
_____
_____
_____
_____
_____
_____
_____
_____
_____
_____
_____
_____
_____
_____
_____
_____
_____
_____
_____

Before Bed Journal

I think:_____
_____
_____
_____
_____

I need: _____
_____
_____
_____
_____

I feel: _____
_____
_____
_____
_____
_____
_____

Today I:_____
_____
_____
_____
_____

I wish that:_____
_____
_____
_____
_____

The worst part of my day today was: _____
_____
_____
_____

The best part of my day today was: _____
_____
_____
_____

Anything Else I need to sort through: _____

_____
_____
_____
_____
_____
_____
_____
_____
_____
_____
_____
_____
_____
_____
_____
_____
_____
_____
_____
_____
_____
_____
_____
_____
_____
_____
_____
_____
_____
_____
_____
_____
_____
_____
_____
_____
_____
_____

Before Bed Journal

I think:_____

_____

_____

_____

_____

I need: _____

_____

_____

_____

_____

I feel: _____

_____

_____

_____

_____

_____

_____

Today I:_____

_____

_____

_____

_____

I wish that:_____

_____

_____

_____

_____

The worst part of my day today was: _____

_____

_____

_____

The best part of my day today was: _____

_____

_____

_____

Anything Else I need to sort through: _____
_____
_____
_____
_____
_____
_____
_____
_____
_____
_____
_____
_____
_____
_____
_____
_____
_____
_____
_____
_____
_____
_____
_____
_____
_____
_____
_____
_____
_____
_____
_____
_____
_____
_____
_____
_____
_____
_____
_____

Before Bed Journal

I think:_____

_____

_____

_____

_____

I need: _____

_____

_____

_____

_____

I feel: _____

_____

_____

_____

_____

_____

_____

Today I:_____

_____

_____

_____

_____

I wish that:_____

_____

_____

_____

_____

The worst part of my day today was: _____

_____

_____

_____

The best part of my day today was: _____

_____

_____

_____

Anything Else I need to sort through: _____
_____
_____
_____
_____
_____
_____
_____
_____
_____
_____
_____
_____
_____
_____
_____
_____
_____
_____
_____
_____
_____
_____
_____
_____
_____
_____
_____
_____
_____
_____
_____
_____
_____
_____
_____
_____
_____
_____
_____
_____
_____
_____
_____
_____

Automatic Thought Log

1. What are you feeling?_____
_____
_____
_____
_____
_____
_____

2. On a scale from 1-10, how strong are these feelings?_____

3. Give three thoughts that are triggering these feelings?_____
_____
_____
_____
_____
_____
_____
_____

4. For each of these statements, what is absolutely true?_____
_____
_____
_____

5. How do you know that's true?_____
_____
_____
_____
_____
_____
_____

6. Are there any thoughts here that might not be true?_____
_____
_____
_____
_____
_____
_____

7. How do you know that these thoughts might not be true?_____

_____

_____

_____

_____

_____

_____

8. What is a more balanced truth here?_____

_____

_____

_____

_____

_____

_____

9. What kind of cognitive distortion is this? _____

_____

_____

_____

_____

_____

_____

10. How are you feeling now?_____

_____

_____

_____

_____

_____

11. On a scale from 1-10, how strong are these feelings now?_____

Automatic Thought Log

1. What are you feeling?_____
_____
_____
_____
_____
_____
_____

2. On a scale from 1-10, how strong are these feelings?_____

3. Give three thoughts that are triggering these feelings?_____
_____
_____
_____
_____
_____
_____

4. For each of these statements, what is absolutely true?_____
_____
_____
_____

5. How do you know that's true?_____
_____
_____
_____
_____
_____
_____

6. Are there any thoughts here that might not be true?_____
_____
_____
_____
_____
_____
_____

7. How do you know that these thoughts might not be true?_____
_____
_____
_____
_____
_____
_____

8. What is a more balanced truth here?_____
_____
_____
_____
_____
_____
_____

9. What kind of cognitive distortion is this? _____
_____
_____
_____
_____
_____

10. How are you feeling now?_____
_____
_____
_____
_____
_____

11. On a scale from 1-10, how strong are these feelings now?_____

Automatic Thought Log

1. What are you feeling?_____
_____
_____
_____
_____
_____

2. On a scale from 1-10, how strong are these feelings?_____

3. Give three thoughts that are triggering these feelings?_____
_____
_____
_____
_____
_____
_____

4. For each of these statements, what is absolutely true?_____
_____
_____
_____

5. How do you know that's true?_____
_____
_____
_____
_____
_____
_____

6. Are there any thoughts here that might not be true?_____
_____
_____
_____
_____
_____
_____

7. How do you know that these thoughts might not be true?_____

_____

_____

_____

_____

_____

_____

8. What is a more balanced truth here?_____

_____

_____

_____

_____

_____

_____

9. What kind of cognitive distortion is this? _____

_____

_____

_____

_____

_____

_____

10. How are you feeling now?_____

_____

_____

_____

_____

_____

_____

11. On a scale from 1-10, how strong are these feelings now?_____

Automatic Thought Log

1. What are you feeling?_____
_____
_____
_____
_____
_____
_____

2. On a scale from 1-10, how strong are these feelings?_____

3. Give three thoughts that are triggering these feelings?_____
_____
_____
_____
_____
_____
_____

4. For each of these statements, what is absolutely true?_____
_____
_____
_____

5. How do you know that's true?_____
_____
_____
_____
_____
_____

6. Are there any thoughts here that might not be true?_____
_____
_____
_____
_____
_____

7. How do you know that these thoughts might not be true?_____

_____

_____

_____

_____

_____

_____

8. What is a more balanced truth here?_____

_____

_____

_____

_____

_____

_____

9. What kind of cognitive distortion is this? _____

_____

_____

_____

_____

_____

_____

10. How are you feeling now?_____

_____

_____

_____

_____

_____

11. On a scale from 1-10, how strong are these feelings now?_____

Automatic Thought Log

1. What are you feeling?_____
_____
_____
_____
_____
_____
_____

2. On a scale from 1-10, how strong are these feelings?_____

3. Give three thoughts that are triggering these feelings?_____
_____
_____
_____
_____
_____
_____
_____

4. For each of these statements, what is absolutely true?_____
_____
_____
_____

5. How do you know that's true?_____
_____
_____
_____
_____
_____
_____

6. Are there any thoughts here that might not be true?_____
_____
_____
_____
_____
_____
_____

7. How do you know that these thoughts might not be true?_____

_____

_____

_____

_____

_____

_____

8. What is a more balanced truth here?_____

_____

_____

_____

_____

_____

_____

9. What kind of cognitive distortion is this? _____

_____

_____

_____

_____

_____

_____

10. How are you feeling now?_____

_____

_____

_____

_____

_____

_____

11. On a scale from 1-10, how strong are these feelings now?_____

Automatic Thought Log

1. What are you feeling?_____
_____
_____
_____
_____
_____
_____

2. On a scale from 1-10, how strong are these feelings?_____

3. Give three thoughts that are triggering these feelings?_____
_____
_____
_____
_____
_____
_____

4. For each of these statements, what is absolutely true?_____
_____
_____
_____

5. How do you know that's true?_____
_____
_____
_____
_____
_____
_____

6. Are there any thoughts here that might not be true?_____
_____
_____
_____
_____
_____
_____

7. How do you know that these thoughts might not be true?_____

_____

_____

_____

_____

_____

_____

8. What is a more balanced truth here?_____

_____

_____

_____

_____

_____

_____

9. What kind of cognitive distortion is this? _____

_____

_____

_____

_____

_____

_____

10. How are you feeling now?_____

_____

_____

_____

_____

_____

_____

11. On a scale from 1-10, how strong are these feelings now?_____

Automatic Thought Log

1. What are you feeling?_____
_____
_____
_____
_____
_____
_____

2. On a scale from 1-10, how strong are these feelings?_____

3. Give three thoughts that are triggering these feelings?_____
_____
_____
_____
_____
_____
_____

4. For each of these statements, what is absolutely true?_____
_____
_____
_____

5. How do you know that's true?_____
_____
_____
_____
_____
_____
_____

6. Are there any thoughts here that might not be true?_____
_____
_____
_____
_____
_____
_____

7. How do you know that these thoughts might not be true?_____

_____

_____

_____

_____

_____

_____

8. What is a more balanced truth here?_____

_____

_____

_____

_____

_____

_____

9. What kind of cognitive distortion is this? _____

_____

_____

_____

_____

_____

_____

10. How are you feeling now?_____

_____

_____

_____

_____

_____

_____

11. On a scale from 1-10, how strong are these feelings now?_____

Automatic Thought Log

1. What are you feeling?_____

_____

_____

_____

_____

_____

_____

2. On a scale from 1-10, how strong are these feelings?_____

3. Give three thoughts that are triggering these feelings?_____

_____

_____

_____

_____

_____

_____

4. For each of these statements, what is absolutely true?_____

_____

_____

_____

5. How do you know that's true?_____

_____

_____

_____

_____

_____

_____

6. Are there any thoughts here that might not be true?_____

_____

_____

_____

_____

_____

_____

7. How do you know that these thoughts might not be true?_____

_____

_____

_____

_____

_____

_____

8. What is a more balanced truth here?_____

_____

_____

_____

_____

_____

_____

9. What kind of cognitive distortion is this? _____

_____

_____

_____

_____

_____

_____

10. How are you feeling now?_____

_____

_____

_____

_____

_____

_____

11. On a scale from 1-10, how strong are these feelings now?_____

Automatic Thought Log

1. What are you feeling?_____

_____

_____

_____

_____

_____

_____

2. On a scale from 1-10, how strong are these feelings?_____

3. Give three thoughts that are triggering these feelings?_____

_____

_____

_____

_____

_____

_____

4. For each of these statements, what is absolutely true?_____

_____

_____

_____

5. How do you know that's true?_____

_____

_____

_____

_____

_____

_____

6. Are there any thoughts here that might not be true?_____

_____

_____

_____

_____

_____

_____

7. How do you know that these thoughts might not be true?_____

_____
_____
_____
_____
_____
_____

8. What is a more balanced truth here?_____

_____
_____
_____
_____
_____
_____

9. What kind of cognitive distortion is this? _____

_____
_____
_____
_____
_____
_____

10. How are you feeling now?_____

_____
_____
_____
_____
_____
_____

11. On a scale from 1-10, how strong are these feelings now?_____

Automatic Thought Log

1. What are you feeling?_____
_____
_____
_____
_____
_____
_____

2. On a scale from 1-10, how strong are these feelings?_____

3. Give three thoughts that are triggering these feelings?_____
_____
_____
_____
_____
_____
_____
_____

4. For each of these statements, what is absolutely true?_____
_____
_____
_____

5. How do you know that's true?_____
_____
_____
_____
_____
_____
_____

6. Are there any thoughts here that might not be true?_____
_____
_____
_____
_____
_____
_____

7. How do you know that these thoughts might not be true?_____

_____

_____

_____

_____

_____

_____

8. What is a more balanced truth here?_____

_____

_____

_____

_____

_____

_____

9. What kind of cognitive distortion is this? _____

_____

_____

_____

_____

_____

_____

10. How are you feeling now?_____

_____

_____

_____

_____

_____

_____

11. On a scale from 1-10, how strong are these feelings now?_____

Inner Critic Worksheet

Date & Time:_____

Event or Trigger (what happened):_____
_____
_____
_____
_____
_____
_____

What my Critic Said:_____
_____
_____
_____
_____
_____

How that Made Me Feel:_____
_____
_____
_____
_____
_____

How I reacted or behaved in reaction to this:_____
_____
_____
_____
_____
_____
_____
_____
_____
_____
_____
_____

Inner Critic Worksheet

Date & Time:_____

Event or Trigger (what happened):_____
_____
_____
_____
_____
_____
_____

What my Critic Said:_____
_____
_____
_____
_____
_____

How that Made Me Feel:_____
_____
_____
_____
_____
_____

How I reacted or behaved in reaction to this:_____
_____
_____
_____
_____
_____
_____
_____
_____
_____
_____

Inner Critic Worksheet

Date & Time:_____

Event or Trigger (what happened):_____

_____

_____

_____

_____

_____

_____

What my Critic Said:_____

_____

_____

_____

_____

_____

How that Made Me Feel:_____

_____

_____

_____

_____

_____

_____

How I reacted or behaved in reaction to this:_____

_____

_____

_____

_____

_____

_____

_____

_____

_____

_____

Inner Critic Worksheet

Date & Time:_____

Event or Trigger (what happened):_____

_____

_____

_____

_____

_____

_____

What my Critic Said:_____

_____

_____

_____

_____

_____

How that Made Me Feel:_____

_____

_____

_____

_____

_____

How I reacted or behaved in reaction to this:_____

_____

_____

_____

_____

_____

_____

_____

_____

_____

_____

Inner Critic Worksheet

Date & Time:_____

Event or Trigger (what happened):_____
_____
_____
_____
_____
_____
_____

What my Critic Said:_____
_____
_____
_____
_____
_____

How that Made Me Feel:_____
_____
_____
_____
_____
_____

How I reacted or behaved in reaction to this:_____
_____
_____
_____
_____
_____
_____
_____
_____
_____
_____

Inner Critic Worksheet

Date & Time:_____

Event or Trigger (what happened):_____
_____
_____
_____
_____
_____
_____

What my Critic Said:_____
_____
_____
_____
_____
_____

How that Made Me Feel:_____
_____
_____
_____
_____
_____
_____

How I reacted or behaved in reaction to this:_____
_____
_____
_____
_____
_____
_____
_____
_____
_____
_____
_____

Inner Critic Worksheet

Date & Time:_____

Event or Trigger (what happened):_____
_____
_____
_____
_____
_____
_____

What my Critic Said:_____
_____
_____
_____
_____
_____

How that Made Me Feel:_____
_____
_____
_____
_____
_____
_____

How I reacted or behaved in reaction to this:_____
_____
_____
_____
_____
_____
_____
_____
_____
_____
_____

Inner Critic Worksheet

Date & Time:_____

Event or Trigger (what happened):_____
_____
_____
_____
_____
_____
_____

What my Critic Said:_____
_____
_____
_____
_____
_____

How that Made Me Feel:_____
_____
_____
_____
_____
_____

How I reacted or behaved in reaction to this:_____
_____
_____
_____
_____
_____
_____
_____
_____
_____
_____
_____

Inner Critic Worksheet

Date & Time:_____

Event or Trigger (what happened):_____
_____
_____
_____
_____
_____
_____

What my Critic Said:_____
_____
_____
_____
_____
_____

How that Made Me Feel:_____
_____
_____
_____
_____
_____

How I reacted or behaved in reaction to this:_____
_____
_____
_____
_____
_____
_____
_____
_____
_____
_____

Inner Critic Worksheet

Date & Time:_____

Event or Trigger (what happened):_____

_____
_____
_____
_____
_____
_____

What my Critic Said:_____

_____
_____
_____
_____
_____

How that Made Me Feel:_____

_____
_____
_____
_____
_____
_____

How I reacted or behaved in reaction to this:_____

_____
_____
_____
_____
_____
_____
_____
_____
_____
_____
_____

Inner Critic Worksheet

Date & Time:_____

Event or Trigger (what happened):_____
_____
_____
_____
_____
_____
_____

What my Critic Said:_____
_____
_____
_____
_____
_____
_____

How that Made Me Feel:_____
_____
_____
_____
_____
_____
_____

How I reacted or behaved in reaction to this:_____
_____
_____
_____
_____
_____
_____
_____
_____
_____
_____
_____
_____

Affirmation Maker

The Goal You Want to Accomplish	The Affirmation to Help you Get there	The Eventual Affirmation

Affirmation Maker

The Goal You Want to Accomplish	The Affirmation to Help you Get there	The Eventual Affirmation

Affirmations

1. My body deserves love

2. I am perfect, whole, and complete just the way I am

3. I feed my body healthy nourishing food and give it healthy nourishing exercise because it deserves to be taken care of

4. I love and respect myself

5. It's okay to love myself now as I continue to evolve

6. My body is a temple. I want to treat it with love and respect.

7. My body is a gift.

8. Food doesn't have to be the enemy, it can be nurturing and healing.

9. Life is too short and too precious to waste time obsessing about my body. I am going to take care of it to the best of my ability and get out of my head and into the world.

10. I will not give in to the voices of my eating disorder that tell me I'm not okay. I will listen to the healthy voices that I do have, even if they are very quiet so that I can understand that I am fine. I am fine.

11. Food doesn't make me feel better, it just temporarily stops me from feeling what I'm feeling.

12. I have everything inside of me that I need to take care of myself without using food.

13. A goal weight is an arbitrary number, how I feel is what's important.

14. I am worthy of love

15. As long as I am good, kind, and hold myself with integrity, it doesn't matter what other people think of me.

16. Other people are too busy thinking about themselves to care what my weight is

17. When I compare myself to others, I destroy myself, I don't want to destroy myself so I'll just continue on my journey, not worrying about other people's journeys.

18. I am blessed to be aging. The only alternative to aging is death.

19. It's okay for me to like myself. It's okay for me to love myself.

20. I have to be an advocate for me. I can't rely on anyone else to do that for me.

21. A "perfect" body is one that works.

22. It's okay for me to trust the wisdom of my body.

23. Just because someone looks perfect on the outside, doesn't mean they have a perfect life. No one has a perfect life, we all struggle. That's just what being human is.

24. If I spend too much time trying to be and look like someone else, I cease to pay attention to myself, my virtues, my path, and my journey.

25. When I look to others to dictate who I should be or how I should look, I reject who I am.

26. The last thing I should be doing is rejecting myself. Accepting myself as I am right now is the first step in changing, growing and evolving. When I reject myself, I cannot grow.

27. Self respect is underrated.

28. I can only go forward, so although I can learn from it, I refuse to dwell on the past.

29. ALL images in magazines are airbrushed, photoshopped, and distorted.

30. If people actively judge or insult me, it's because they feel badly about themselves. No one who feels good about themselves has the need to put someone down to elevate themselves- they have better things to do with their time.

31. I have no need to put someone down to elevate myself.

32. I can be a good person if I choose to be.

33. It's my life, I can choose the way I want to live it.

34. When I smile, I actually make other people happy.

35. Balance is the most important.

36. If I binge today, I can still love and accept myself, I don't have to beat, berate and starve myself right afterwards, and I still have the very next moment to jump right back into recovery.

37. Recovery is an ongoing process that is not linear in fashion. If I slip up, I'll take the opportunity as a learning experience and get right back to my recovery goals/program.

38. Progress is not linear. It's normal for me to go forward and then backward, and then forward again.

39. I enjoy feeling good. It's okay for me to feel good.

40. Having an eating disorder is not my identity.

41. Being skinny or fat is not my identity. I am identified by who I am on the inside, a loving, wonderful person.

42. I choose health and healing over diets and punishing myself.

43. My opinion of myself is the only one I truly know and it's the only one that counts. I can choose my opinion of myself.

44. When I am in my head too much, I can return to my breath, just breath and be okay. There is only this moment.

45. It's okay to let others love me, why wouldn't they?

46. I am good stuff.

47. I am compassionate and warm. My presence is delightful to people.

48. My very existence makes the world a better place.

49. It's okay to pay someone to rub my feet every once in a while.

50. If I am hungry, I am supposed to let myself eat. Food is what keeps me alive.

51. Getting older makes me smarter.

52. It's okay not to be the best all the time.

53. My well-being is the most important thing to me. I am responsible for taking care of me. We are each responsible for ourselves.

54. No one has the power to make me feel bad about myself without my permission.

55. My feet are cute. Even if they're ugly.

56. I eat for energy and nourishment.

57. Chocolate is not the enemy. It's not my friend either. It's just chocolate, it has no power over me.

58. I can be conscious in my choices.

59. I am stronger than the urge to binge.

60. I am healthier than the urge to purge.

61. Restricting my food doesn't make me a better person, being kind to myself and to others makes me a better person.

62. Being skinny doesn't make me good. Being fat doesn't make me bad.

63. I can be healthy at any size.

64. Life doesn't start 10 pounds from now, it's already started. I can make the choice to include myself in it.

65. Food, drugs, and alcohol are not the solution. But they might seem like it at times, but using these things can make more problems. I have what I need inside of me as the solution.

66. There is a guide inside of me who is wise and will always be there to help me on my journey.

67. Sometimes sitting around and doing nothing is just what the doctor ordered. It's okay to let myself relax.

68. I am a human being, not a human doing. It's okay to *just be* sometimes. I don't always have to be doing.

69. My brain is my sexiest body part.

70. Looks last about five minutes– or until someone opens their mouth.

71. My life is what I make of it. I have all the power here.

72. My body is a vessel for my awesomeness.

73. My body can do awesome things.

74. If I am healthy, I am so very blessed.

75. I won't let magazines or the media tell me what I should look like. I look exactly the way I'm supposed to. I know because this is the way god made me!

76. What is *supposedly* pleasing to the eye is not always what is pleasing to the touch. Cuddly is good!

77. I can trust my intuition. It's here to guide me.

78. Just because I am taking care of myself and being an advocate for myself doesn't mean I'm selfish.

79. Not everyone has to like me. I just have to like me.

80. It's not about working on myself it's about being okay with who I already am.

81. My needs are just as important as anyone else.

82. Body, if you can love me for who I am, I promise to love you for who you are– no one is responsible for changing anyone else.

83. I will make peace with my body, it doesn't do anything but keep me alive and all I do is insult it and hurt it. I'm sorry body, you've tried to be good to me and care for me, it's time for me to try to be good back.

84. Thighs, thank you for carrying me.

85. Belly, thank you for holding in all my organs and helping me digest.

86. Skin, thank you for shielding and protecting me.

87. Other people don't dictate my choices for me, I know what's best for myself.

88. I feed my body life affirming foods so that I can be healthy and vital.

89. Taking care of myself feels good.

90. I can eat a variety of foods for health and wellness without bingeing.

91. There is more to life that losing weight. I'm ready to experience it.

92. If I let go of my obsession with food and my body weight, there is a whole world waiting for me to explore.

93. The numbers on the scale are irrelevant to who I am as a human.

94. Food is not good or bad. It has no moral significance. I can choose to be good or bad and it has nothing to do with the amount of calories or carbohydrates I eat.

95. I am still beautiful when I'm having a bad hair day.

96. My nose gives me the ability to breathe. Breath gives me the ability to be an amazingly grounded, solid person.

97. Being grounded and whole is what makes me beautiful. If I don't feel grounded and whole, I can get there just by being still, breathing, listening to my intuition, and doing what I can to be kind to myself and others.

98. I am not bad and I don't deserve to be punished, not by myself and not by others.

99. I deserve to be treated with love and respect and so do you. I choose to do and say kind things for and about myself and for and about others.

100. Even if I don't see how pretty I am, there is someone who does. I am loved and admired. REALLY!

101. Beauty?... To me it is a word without sense because I do not know where its meaning comes from nor where it leads to. ~Pablo Picasso

"You will only ever live the life you create for yourself.

Your life is yours alone. Others can try to persuade you, but they can't decide for you. They can walk with you, but not in your shoes. So make sure the path you decide to walk aligns with your own intuition and desires, and don't be scared to switch paths or pave a new one when it makes sense.

Remember, it's always better to be at the bottom of the ladder you want to climb than the top of the one you don't. Be productive and patient. And realize that patience is not about waiting, but the ability to keep a good attitude while working hard for what you believe in. This is your life, and it is made up entirely of your choices. May your actions speak louder than your words. May your life preach louder than your lips. May your success be your noise in the end..." Marc & Angel

Made in the USA
Lexington, KY
21 September 2015